It's Spritz O'Clock Somewhere

Rick Lupert

Bologna, Florence, Naples and Paris

It's Spritz O'clock Somewhere

Copyright © 2024 by Rick Lupert
All rights reserved

Ain't Got No Press

Design, Layout, Photography ~ Rick Lupert

This book is protected under the copyright laws of the United States of America. Any reproduction or other unauthorized use of the material or artwork herein is prohibited without the express written permission of the author except in the case of brief quotations embodied in critical articles and reviews.

First Edition ~ May, 2024

ISBN-13: 978-1-7330278-4-7

Visit the author online at
www.PoetrySuperHighway.com

The best way to die is sit under a tree, eat lots of bologna and salami, drink a case of beer, then blow up.

— Art Donovan

I've always considered Florence as my girlfriend. I don't have to explain my love for this city.

— Gabriel Batistuta

People in the U.S. are more reserved, whereas in Naples they'll hit each other and then kiss each other a second after.

— Lucy Devito

Paris is always a good idea.

— Audrey Hepburn

Thank you Addie, Jude, Brendan, Elizabeth, Rachel, Heidi, Allesandro, Fabrizio, The Thread, and the many people who made food and drinks which we put in our mouths.

The poem "Not Ordinary" (page 317) first appeared in the *Sparring With Beatnik Ghosts* anthology, September, 2023.

The poems "At Night With Pizza" (page 247) and "Paris Is the Dream" (page 341) first appeared in *Dashboard Horus,* April 10, 2024.

For Addie, who is the best possible spritz partner

Aperitif

a time before we went
and then we went

The Gelato Department

I tell Addie she's in charge of Gelato
two weeks before we leave the American ground.
I've been arranging all the other details —

where we're going to sleep, what we're
going to do between the times when we sleep
what we're going to put in our mouths.

I just discovered you can search for
Michelin Star restaurants and now am
going to have to mortgage our house

to eat the way I want to eat on this trip.
But Addie's in charge of gelato.
Though she's not ready to think about it

as she has to leave town and then come back
before we fly over North America and the Atlantic.
I'm sure she's up to the task.

She's the entire gelato department.

We're dropping our kid off at camp tomorrow.

While eating the special Fourth of July brunch
that Addie has prepared while Alexa plays
a John Philip Sousa playlist, Jude asks

*what happens if the Leaning Tower of Pisa
falls over when you're in it?* Now I want to
meet the guy whose responsibility is to

stand at the bottom of the tower and
watch it for signs that it's going to fall over
as people enter it. Better yet, this is the job

I want to have. There are red and white berries
to put on the waffles, plus a white *crème fraîche*.
This is the first sign we are leaving America.

I tell Jude the story of the very first Pisa Tower Watcher
whose father was crushed when it first fell. When one
doesn't know history, making it up is the only option.

We're leaving America on Friday.
But only for a little while. We'll be back —
assuming the tower doesn't fall.

We're dropping our kid off at camp today.

I was as surprised as anyone when
music shuffle put on the overture to
Jesus Christ Superstar at the exact moment
we rolled in to Jewish summer camp
to drop our son off.

We're not going to see him for three weeks
and our hope is he will fully immerse
himself in this experience.

Jesus isn't helping.

Or maybe he meant to chime in
on the day we're going to visit
the Duomo in Florence.

They've got at least two structures
I can climb up to survey what
all the believers have built.

It'll be funny if, the moment our train
arrives there, the soundtrack to *Joseph
and the Amazing Technicolor Dreamcoat*
starts blaring. Maybe that's what Siri
meant to play. She always confuses
Andrew Lloyd Webber productions.

As long as it isn't *Cats* we're in good shape.
That one had a good overture but even with
the appeal of cats it didn't go anywhere.

We're hoping our kid doesn't go anywhere
over the next three weeks, while we go everywhere.

Hosanna, heysanna, sanna, sanna
Hosanna, heysanna, hosanna

Hey, Jude, hey, Jude we'll bring you back
some fusilli, or at least take you to *Eataly*.

You're our superstar.

Awkward Amount of Time Thoughts

I
There is an awkward amount of time between
when I woke up and when the Lyft is coming
to take us to the airport. Normally when we go,
we go early in the morning. This 4:18 p.m. flight
to London is messing with everything I know
about when to go places.

II
Also, I'm concerned about the tight connection
between flights at Heathrow. If we don't make it
look forward to my epic poem called *Eight Hours
of Observations in the London Airport.*

III
This trip doesn't overlap with the 4th of July
so there's no need to pack my red, white,
and blue American flag underwear, but I
didn't want to not mention it at all for
those of you who like through lines.

This Poem Was Written Merely for Entertainment Purposes and Is Not an Admission That I Dye My Hair

I tell Addie I have to decide whether to dye
and shave off all my hair, but she hears *die*
and asks me to not.

Anything for you, my love.

How Are We Checking Our Luggage on the Way Back?

We're not checking luggage on the way
to Italy because our connecting flight is tight
and we don't want to end up naked in Bologna.
But on the way back, with a direct flight,
anything goes and Addie declares
we can check the fuck out of our luggage.
I'm sorry you had to read that out of
such sweet lips.

Thoughts in a Lyft

I
Do I have my passport?
Asking for a friend.

II
Addie is practicing Italian
in the ride to the airport.
So far she's able to say
one moment please and
*would you like cream
in your coffee.* So those
are two less things to
worry about.

Hello Pilot

I'd like to talk to the pilot
to see if he's willing to fly
a little faster so our connection
in London is a little easier.
Like when I'm on the treadmill
and I set the speed to two tenths
miles per hour faster so I can
get my steps in less time.

I'd like to talk to the pilot
about how he just said there's
a magnificent view of the
Grand Canyon on the left side
of the plane and we're on the right.
Would he be willing to circle
around so it's fair for everyone?

I'd like to talk to the pilot
about so many things but
Addie would prefer I didn't.

In Flight

I
We're seated in the front row of
our cabin with two seats just for us
and a lot of extra space. We might
have people over later. That guy in
Premium Economy with the nice
looking salad seems like a good
place to start making friends.

II
The water bottles are square in shape
which is smart so they don't roll off
your tray table. Even so, the square edges
are subtle and they feel nice rolling
across my face.

III
My video screen doesn't work so
get ready for eight hours of observations
about the wall in front of me.

(It would have been ten but I had to wait
for them to clear away my finished meal.)

IV
The Wall in Front of Me...
separates my level of cabin
from the next one.

Shit, that's all I've got.

V
I think we're flying over a Great Lake.
I want to let all the other lakes I know
that I think they're great too.

VI
Addie is extra excited when the map
shows we are flying over Grand Forks
and now she wants a set of them.

VII
I'm kind of turned on when we fly over
Kelvin Seamount but I'm not sure why.

VIII
We are chasing the top of
the earth's curvature of darkness.
I'm sure this would be beautiful
if they let me on top of the plane
to take a look.

IX
The darkness curvature on the map
reminds me of the drawing in
"Le Petit Prince" which was either
a man's hat or a snake that swallowed
an elephant.

X
We're halfway to London
is what I'd like to say but
the map shows me it's less than
a third as Florida sticks out limp
into the sea.

XI
I'm over Canada now.
I guess this is better than
being under Canada.

XII
I'm going to try to get some sleep
so if you could close the book quietly
I'll catch up with you in a few hours
on the next page.

XIII
Good morning!
Just kidding.
It's only a few minutes later.
I find it impossible to
sleep on airplanes.

XIV
There are seven different slides
rotating on the main cabin display.
Five of them are different maps.
Two of them are text-based with
information such as our *true air speed*.
This would be fascinating if
my seat screen was working and
I didn't have to look at these seven slides
for ten hours and seven minutes.

XV
I just realized my seatbelt
hasn't been fastened for
the last two hours.
Why didn't you guys
say anything?

XVI
P.S. Our true air speed
is 558 miles per hour.
I hope we don't get
pulled over.

XVII
Somehow it became
night and day on this plane while
my eyes never closed.

XVIII
I asked Jude if writing him
every day was too much.
Not enough he said.
I don't know if that's true
but it was the right answer.

XIX
An area of the Atlantic Ocean
to the east of Ireland is called
Porcupine Bank. I'm not sure
if this is where one goes to
deposit their porcupines or
if this is where porcupines
do their banking. Either way
I hear the interest rates
fluctuate sharply.

XX
I'll say this about ten hours of
the same seven screens of
maps and flight information:
No commercials.

XXI
You gotta lick the yogurt film
is a truth I never expected
Addie to drop on me at
31,000 feet or any altitude
really.

P.S. Mark this off as one of the things she
didn't want me to include in this book.

XXII
What Addie said after I asked her
if she wanted the other fruit cup:

Long pause and look of disbelief.

No.
I do not want the fruit cup.
I don't want to think about the fruit cup.
I regret opening the fruit cup.

XXIII
I hear it gets off the hook
at the Charlie-Gibbs
Fracture Zone.

XXIV
I'm not even going to
say anything about
Josephine Seamount.

England, Briefly

I
Heathrow is a haphazard
pigeon fuck of an airport.

II
This flight to Bologna —
the seats are so close together
it's like they duct taped me
to the people in front of me.

III
Goodbye England.
I didn't even have a sip of your water
and I'm already leaving your ground.
It's not how I like to do it. But this time,
it wasn't meant to be.

IV
Addie doesn't mind sitting
in the middle seat as there's
a fresh baby she can make
eye contact with sitting
one row ahead.

V
So many British Airways planes
in line to go where they're going.
You could probably look up the schedule.
I don't have all the information.

VI
A *Eurowings* plane is parked
next to ours in Bologna.
Or it's a cleverly placed
themed chicken place.

An Evening in Bologna

Step One in Bologna

Don't expect the restaurants
to be labeled *Italian food*.
They just call it *food* here.

Step Two in Bologna

A transportation strike today
is making it take as long as
The Roman Empire to get
to our hotel.

Step Three in Bologna

Everyone smokes in Italy
except for the people who don't
but I'm not sure who those people are.

Italian Food

We may have already overindulged in
everything that Italy has to offer with just one meal.

Complimentary appetizers, wine, bread
and then, of course, we ordered food.

It was just what we needed to orient our
stomachs to this way of life after the

terrible transition of the day.
We're going to sleep forever.

I'm talking Rip Van Winkle amounts of sleep.
My phone doesn't even know what day it is.

Both our heads and our two sets of feet
have said they're striking tomorrow in solidarity

with the transportation workers.
I salute their efforts.

Speaking of sleep,

our hotel room is right next to Piazza Maggiore
which is great in terms of location.

Except when 2,500 people gather every night
for the open air cinema. We can hear the movie

in our room. It's a gift of sorts.
A reminder of home.

Bologna Day 1

in which we leave Bologna and go to Modena

L'Orologio

The bell in the clock tower for which
this hotel is named, rings two sets of times.

When it is eight o'clock, the bell will ring
eight times, then a few minutes later

will ring eight more. This ancient snooze
system surpasses the need for a digital age

but doesn't prevent me from asking Addie
is it ten o'clock? thinking we have overslept.

It is eight o'clock she responds. *But there were
ten bells* I tell her. *There were eight bells*

she tells me. We have not overslept and
I have lost the ability to count to ten

on this vacation. This feels right to me as
no one should have to commingle with numbers

when work is thousands of miles away.

Close Shave

I left my razor in Los Angeles and have to
send Addie down to the front desk
as I'm in no condition to be visible
to human beings who aren't her
to ask for one. Either that or agree to
go full *Zach Singer* for the duration
of the trip. Just so you feel included,
though you may have guessed,
Zach Singer is a person I know
with a mighty beard. Addie agrees
to seek out a razor and the woman
has one but also says *but we don't
have the cream*. I'm not sure how
exactly Addie reacted to that but
I'm sure, deep in her psyche,
with her intimate knowledge of me
she knew I already had the cream.

Some mornings

like this one
I have to lube up
my finger to be
able to slide my
wedding ring on.
They call me *Mister
Fat Fingered Man*
in Bologna, Italy
with my occasionally
fat finger.

At Breakfast

I
He insists we have cappuccinos
this morning, the man who
seats us at breakfast. As far
as we know he's in charge
of all our decisions today.

II
They bring Addie a basket
of gluten-free delights which
reminds her who she is
and makes her feel better
about her departure from
that lifestyle for the rest
of our Italian days.

III
This is the best cappuccino
I've had in Italy since
before the war.

IV
Frizzante means *frizzy*
I learn as the unexpected
bubbles travel down
my esophagus.

Five Ages of Parmesan Cheese

I'm on my first Italian train
heading to Modena which I
learned about on the television.
Five ages of Parmesan cheese
are in my future; Addie's too.
Conceived by Massimo, the wild-
haired Italian native who, at first,
the locals didn't want.
Now you can visit his restaurants
all over the world, even back at home
which could have saved us
having to set foot in Heathrow.
But this is where it started.
This town. This cheese.
This wild man.

This Train

I
The train door
closed on Addie.
How dare it?

II
Prego means *you're welcome*
or is at least the typical response
to *grazie* which means *thank you*.
It also rhymes with *Lego* which
means colored brick that you
stick to other *colored brick*, which
is all I can think about as we
walked by the Lego Store to the train.

III
That poor train I think
as we roll by a line car
graffitied, on another track
by itself. Where are its friends
or what did it do to find itself
in this situation?

IV
Addie's looking forward to our
stop at Pavarotti's house and museum.
I hope this isn't the day of all mute tours
I tell her, which reminds her of the
time we didn't go to the Corvette Museum
in Tennessee as that's the day
a sinkhole had sucked up
all the corvettes.

V
How many tenors are left
Addie wonders. *Let's count
them as we encounter them*
I think but don't tell her as
there's only so much of my
whole thing I should
bombard her with.

VI
P.S. Pavarotti is dead.
But that doesn't mean
he won't be home.

Luciano Pavarotti of Modena

I
He would give free singing lessons
in this room, using this piano.

II
He would clutch his famous
handkerchief jutting out of his
tuxedo pocket to deal with
the lack of movement from
the choreographed operas
he was used to.

III
Pavarotti's cell phone and playing cards
His *Mont Blanc* fountain pen
His paint brushes and doodles
Pavarotti's yellow kitchen and ice maker
Pavarotti's collection of Russian nesting dolls
This man with his world famous voice
was a man like any of us.

Pavarotti's Grammys and Emmys
His city keys and sculptures made of him
His platinum albums
His ceremonial shovel given to him by the Prince of Wales
He was also a super man just like
The Bonos and Celine Dions he commingled with.

IV
He sang *Ave Maria*
with Bono which is
weird and wonderful.

V
Addie wants to know who the fourth
of the three tenors was.

VI
I'm in Pavarotti's bedroom.
Don't get any ideas.

VII
Pavarotti's DVD collection includes
*Life is Beautiful, Stripes, Happy Gilmore,
La Sposa de Chucky*
among many others.

VIII
Pavarotti's hand towels and bidet and sauna.

IX
There was a genuine joy on his face
when people would applaud.
He seemed astonished and
so grateful.

The greatest singer alive.

X
The unpublished videos
of Pavarotti backstage
Pavarotti rehearsing
Pavarotti combing his hair
Pavarotti singing with his friends
What a human man.

XI
The Italian countryside
outside Pavarotti's
upstairs windows.

XII
Doesn't everyone have
an Italian elevator
in their house?

XIII
"People think I'm disciplined. It is not discipline.
It's devotion. There is a great difference."
　　　~Luciano Pavarotti

XIV
Can I have your hand
Addie asks, wanting help up.
Take my hand.
Take my whole life too.

XV
The people who knew him
called him *Luciano*.

XVI
Luciano kissed
Stevie on the
forehead.

XVII
Trying to determine if I
should carry around
a handkerchief and wave
it around like Pavarotti
in all situations.

Mythology

When Addie's cute little fork
falls off the table twice and she
wonders how that happened
I regale her with the tale of
the Italian Jumping Forks.

Truth

Spaghetti is the Italian word for *spaghetti*.

Enzo Ferrari Museum

I
I see a car without its metal shell
which I dub *the naked Ferrari*.

II
Most cars we judge
on whether or not we can
fit our guitars in the trunk.

So far it's a *no* and we're
having a hard time justifying the price.

III
In 1947
Ferrari described
his first race as a
promising failure.

IV
He was a ferocious advocate of
the religion of work.

A Walk Around Modena

I
Now, every time we hear clock bells
in any town, I ask if it's ten o'clock.

II
Italians of any age
smoke like they're
going to live forever
as they slowly kill us.

III
The tower in the Piazza Grande
also looks like it's leaning, but
not so much as to make it famous
like the one in Pisa.

A Parade in Modena

A parade of formally dressed Italians
in red vests with whips breaks out near Piazza Grande.
I guess there's a marching band too.

It looks like it might be dueling parades as a
German-looking marching band just walked by the other way.
Also, they may not be Germans.

Anyway, I hope they fight because we've
got a couple hours until dinner and nothing to do.
Around the corner yet another parade is playing

American patriotic music and we think
we may be catching the tail end of World War II.
Turns out it was a Ukrainian band.

The not-German band just started playing
a Simon and Garfunkel song.
Looks like the whip crackers are marching away.

Then Addie's dress almost fell off
and we had to change directions.

At Benny's Bar

I
The barber pole straws in
my first ever Apérol Spritz
remind me of Venice gondolas
and make me the happiest
boy in Modena. It's also
possible whatever is in
this drink is contributing
to my happiness.

II
Does Elephant Gin
contain real elephant?

III
A guy grabs a chair all the way
across Benny's bar and I shout
I'm using that but he either doesn't
hear me, speak English, or care.

Osteria Francescana

I'd like to tell you about
what it's like to eat at
Osteria Francescana in Modena

but I'm in the food-induced
coma set on by the twelve
courses of food they brought us.

(Plus the extra cheese course
with only two ingredients:
cheese and time.)

Think of your favorite artist.
Now apply their sensibility and skill
to the creation of food.

That's a start. It was formal and
expensive. It was so much. We
probably won't eat again for

two weeks. That's a lie, of course,
because that's not how bodies work.
Our bodies are barely working

right now on this train back to
Bologna. The gift of this experience
will keep me alive.

This train was late.

On the one hand we
didn't miss it. On the
other it's already tomorrow.
I've run out of hands to further
examine this experience.

Goodnight Bologna

It's time to say *goodnight* to Bologna again.
Only this time, thanks to a train delay, and

our hotel key ceasing to honor its main function
and, the many, many emails, and, having to

write this so you would know this, it's later
than I want it to be. If only time would go

at the speed I desired, or not at all, sometimes,
if that's how I was feeling.

Pavarotti was the perfect way to start since
we're all about the music. Anything goes

from here on out, especially if it involves food.
Nothing will top what we ate tonight.

Not here. Not anywhere. (Though I'll keep
you up to date on our progress to try.)

We've got a free walking tour up next
after breakfast which comes after sleep.

They say *free* but then the tip-pitch comes.
I've got the local currency in my pocket

because I think they're going to deserve it.
Goodnight, Bologna. My stomach will see you

tomorrow.

Bologna Day 2

in which we do not leave Bologna

Crema

Our new hotel key weighs 25 pounds.
That could be an exaggeration but
I didn't bring a scale with me and I'm
using my morning sensibilities in this
Bologna sun to make a best guess.

Even though I've already had a
double espresso, the length of
last night's meal and the fact that
it's a different time in all the places
I'm used to being in is...

sorry...in the middle of that last
sentence I was brought another espresso
and I have no idea what words
were going to come next.

I believe in honesty. Addie tells me
honestly, I should not drink the
American coffee. I assure her
there will be no American coffee
on this honeymoon. Keep the

espressos coming. Single. Double.
With perfect cremas on top.
I'm easy. Hopefully, the day will be
as easy as my sensibility on
what coffee to drink.

It's an eclectic mix of music in the breakfast room.

Opera into The Rolling Stones.
A song that sounds like
Stevie Wonder, but isn't.
Addie doesn't want to be
mentioned in this poem so
I won't, but I will say that
smooth jazz is never the answer.

Unshirtainty

I'm not sure this is the right shirt
for today, but, honestly, I'm never sure
if any shirt is the right shirt for any day.

Free Walking Tour

I
I don't see anyone who
looks obviously like a guide
in this gathering spot which
teaches me how easy it would be
to be a free tour tour guide.

II
How'd you like to go up this
I ask Addie who is not ready
to go up anything, next to the
tallest tower in Bologna.

III
We're standing on an invisible
underground river.

IV
Travel just one kilometer
in Italy and you change everything —
the pasta, the dialect, the bread.
Everything.

V
All roads lead to Rome.
Except for the ones that don't.

VI
The Spanish Inquisition may have
started as the Bologna Inquisition
centuries earlier.

VII
The two towers square
used to be the five towers square.
You do the math.

VIII
Towers were owned privately
and the height of your tower
was indicative of the amount
of your wealth.

IX
They considered Christians
to be a sect of Judaism.

X
In the Jewish ghetto
the synagogue is on
Via Dell'inferno
Hell Street.

XI
Jews invented a system
to travel between buildings
without going outside.
We were the first people to
innovate against temperatures.

XII
Two months ago it was very cold
and the Italians weren't happy.
Today it is very hot and the Italians
are not happy.

XIII
Solomon said you have to eat history
to digest it.

XIV
We're getting a lot of *Jewish*
on this tour and the guide
even speaks some Hebrew.
I'm going to give him the
secret handshake and see if
he'll give us a discount.

P.S. That's funny because it's a free tour.

XV
When you have a law
everyone will try to find a way
to avoid that law.

XVI
Someone asks if he is Jewish
and he says his mother was.

XVII
All the towers are leaning
but no one wants their autographs.

XVIII
One tower used to be a prison
but don't worry, now it's a B and B.

XIX
Mauritzio or *Maurice* could be our guide's name.
There are too many people asking questions
about Bologna to ever know.

XX
He keeps saying
come, I want to show you something
which is perfect because
we're on this tour because
we want to see things.

XXI
Thanks to their foundations,
during earthquakes,
the towers don't fall.
They dance.

XXII
Italians horde history.
They don't know revolution.
They accept everything.

XXIII
The word *mafia* is Arabic.

XXIV
We have a pornography of food in Bologna.

XXV
Osteria — we go with our wine to eat their food.
Trattoria — we go with our food to drink their wine.

XXVI
Everyone comes to Bologna just to eat.
But don't come to Bologna just to eat.

XXVII
We walked in so many porticos here.
One of them is the longest in the world.
But who has time for that?

XXVIII
Charlie Chaplin loved Bologna.
He spread children all over Europe.

XXIX
The secret long dick of Neptune.

XXX
Addie wants to make sure I'm going to
get a pic of Neptune's secret dick.
I assure her that later it will be all dick pics.

XXXI
One pope cancelled eleven days
because the stars told him to.

XXXII
The hospital and the university
were physically connected so
student doctors would have
bodies to work with.

XXXIII
The word *wine* comes from
the word for *love*.

XXXIV
A few bombs fell down in 1944
explaining the one new building
in the middle of the ancient city.

XXXV
A church became
a cinema
became a bookstore.

XXXVI
The best, and free if you need it, healthcare is here.
They don't have many things here so
when they have something good they have to tell you.

XXXVII
Osteria del Sole (1461) is the
oldest osteria in Bologna. If you've
read carefully, you already know
they only serve wine here.
Bring your own food.

How Decisions Are Made

The biggest decision of the day
is *cheese board* versus *cheese sandwich*.
You can only order a sandwich standing up.
This moment, and our tired post-tour legs,
dictate it will be a cheese board.

At Vecchia Malga

I
There's a ladder to the ceiling
in the bathroom at Vecchia Malga
in case you need to get up there
and do your ceiling business.

II
The boy or girl who broke a glass
stands on top of, and in the middle of,
the glass to clean it up.
You do what you want in Bologna.

III
We can't finish all the cheese which
is a crime against everything I stand for.

IV
The balsamic is thick like ketchup.

V
My friends won't stop messaging me
about how their Bologna has a first name
or second name. Florence, with its
not Bologna name, can't come
soon enough.

VI
Yes, all of Italy,
please come smoke
next to the tables
we are eating at.

VII
Now I'm singing the Oscar Meyer song
over this plate of cheeses.
Damn you Cantor Ross Wolman
from Phoenix.

VIII
I've learned how to say *the check please* —
Il conto, per favore — with such confidence.
But it's often not the right thing as
they keep telling us to leave our table to
pay at the cash register.

IX
Tripdick
The promise
The secret
The sad truth

X
The six o'clock bells ring
and no one is willing to prove to me
that it is not ten o'clock.

XI
Addie has invented the concept of *fluffy meat*
referring to the thin mortadella slices
being delivered to all the other tables.
If we ate meat, surely this would be the
place to do it.

XII
The end of my Apérol Spritz
convinces me I should show a
picture of my cat Bootsy to
our waiter who agrees he's cute
and tells us of the blind cat he used
to live with who also had a broken back.
He's never heard of Bootsy Collins
and only knows James Brown by name
and that's fine. I have other names
of cats pictures I can show him.

XIII
Now I want to ask pedestrians
if they would like to see my cat
or if they would like to see me

lower my lip with my fingers.

That line space before the previous line
was unintentional and another
artifact of the Apérol Spritz.

XIV
Saggy boob meat.

The Grand Square

I want to know how much
Addie will give me if I
get up on the stage in front of
the twenty five hundred people
watching the movie in the
main square and say
il conto, per favore!
The check, please!
She does not give me
an answer.

Not Gelato

A man is yelling at us in Italian
in the cremeria line. Not *us* specifically
but everyone in this line.
I'm not sure what he's saying
but it might be related to
the place not having *gelato*
in the name.

Back in Our Room

Tonight's film in the piazza
features lots of Nazis shouting
so that's a huge help.

448 Steps

I walked up 448 steps today.
Down the same number.

That's led to me finding it
difficult to write this down.

But here it is — all 448 steps
somehow in these words.

I took a nap between
this stanza and the last one.

We're both in the middle of
this poem and I just want

you to know we're in this
together. Hello.

All the towers lean here.
It's their thing.

My thing is to go to sleep
before I have to wake up

which, concerning tomorrow
is so soon, I may not finish

this poem before then.
I better cut out now

just to be safe.

One More Thing

Our walking tour guide
when referring to *World War II*
referred to the German *occupation*
as opposed to acknowledging
Italy was part of the deal.

Bologna Day 3

in which we leave Bologna again

Good Morning Bologna

The Romans built their towns twenty-five miles apart
because that's how far they could march in a day.

We're heading, maybe, two towns away today
(by train so we should arrive before the Romans)

to meet a man (who may or may not be Roman)
who will put cheese, wine, and vinegar in our mouths.

We're not sure of the order of the second two
but it definitely begins with cheese.

This will affect the amount of hotel food we
will put in our own mouths at seven a.m.

(which is in thirty-three minutes) at the very moment
that food is available to us. I'm planning on

another double espresso. If I were to put my
money on it, I'd say Addie was going to get

a cappuccino. They have *American Coffee*
here too, but it is not something you or I want.

This is not the day a cow is supposed to lick me.
Or the city. But today's cheese foreshadows this.

Good morning, Bologna. We're marching to the west
today. Not so far so we'll see the edges of home.

Our Fortune

Did I tell you about all the chairs in the streets
in stacks waiting for restaurants to unstack them
for the day? I tell Addie *we could make our fortune
selling these chairs.* She points out they're chained
together. *That just means we can take them
all at once* I tell her. Addie does not want to
be in the chair selling business.
Who can blame her?

Season One Reference

For various reasons
my thumb hurts but
this is not a new situation
so I'm not sure why I'm
bringing it up now.

Wisdom From Addie

Never put on socks
and walk back into
the bathroom.

At Breakfast

I
I'm trying to read my fortune
at the bottom of my finished
double espresso. It's going
to be a day filled with
espresso swirl residue.

II
I am awake in Italy while
almost everyone I know
is asleep in America.

Train to Reggio Emilia

Things are often easier
than you think they'll be.
Organizing a train ride to
another city while in America
feels like advanced calculus.
But on the ground in Italy
it's as easy as asking for
an espresso.

Stop 1 - Anzola dell'Emilia

I
A few people get off the train.
Did anyone get on?
I can't tell from where
I am sitting.

II
One guy got on I discover
as he takes a seat across from us.

III
Some of the doors on this train
are *out of order* according to the
announcement in Italian, English
and German.

Stop 2 - Samoggia

I
Samoggia is not spelled
like it sounded over the
train audio system.

II
A gaggle of red backhoes
just outside of town.

III
Then a field of sunflowers.

Stop 3 - Castelfranco Emilia

I
I wish this one was called
Castle Frankenstein.

II
If you pee on a high speed train
where are you even peeing?

III
Addie has just learned how to say
we have arrived from Bologna*
which should come in handy
as soon as we get off this train.

*in Italian.

IV
Farmhouses young and old
dot the Italian countryside.

V
How many of these houses were here
when the second war to end all wars
was news and not history.

VI
I don't know where we're arriving next
but that guy is getting off.

Stop 4 - Modena

I
We were here before.
That's something we
can rarely say in
situations like this.

II
Now a tunnel.
What is Italy hiding
between Modena and
wherever is next?

III
Addie stands up and
then sits down. I'm sure
she would agree, no one
needed to know that.

IV
A city of shipping containers
like from a movie which featured
a city of shipping containers.

Stop 5 - Rubiera

I
One more stop
is an observation
which may not
do justice to
this one.

II
If I ran the train
I would get to go
to all the places
for free.

III
We are deep into the area
where they make the things
we are about to eat.

IV
Addie declares she
needs her shoe eraser
which I find alarming.

Stop 6 - Reggio Emilia

I
I don't have time to
tell you anything. I
have to get off the train.

II
The last thing I need is
a receipt for the two euro
it cost to use the toilet
at the train station.

III
Caution
children frolicking
across the street
is, I'm pretty sure,
what that sign is trying
to communicate to me.

Cheese, Balsamic, Wine

Cheese - Caseificio Il Boiardo

I
Boiardo the poet
who wrote the poem *Orlando Furioso*
after which this dairy is named
lost his mind for love.

II
Parmesan Reggiano
is produced every day
because cows don't take
a day off.

III
The cheese here has been DOP
Denominazione di Origine Protetta
(Protected Designation of Origin)
ever since the ocean went away
leaving this land mineral rich and
ripe for cheese.

IV
I ask Allesandro if there will be a test
after he gives us so much information
about the cheese production.

He says *yes, a taste test.*

V
We put on blue plastic suits.
I'm wondering if they have the shoe covers
in a size 7, U.S.

VI
Even the cheese has to pass a test.

VII
Even the cheese needs to breathe.

VIII
There are red cows
but not here.

IX
An old cheese man comes in
and takes a table of things away.

X
The cheese sits in salt water for
twenty-two days before it is cheese.

XI
Let me tell you definitively
you can eat the rind of the cheese.

XII
The aging room is
every smell I've ever wanted.

XIII
Like whiskey
there is also
an angel's share.

XIV
Each wheel is checked by the consortium.
They have to *listen* to each wheel
before the *certified* is burned on.

XV
*We're going to make our fortune
selling wheels of Parmesan cheese*
I tell Addie. They're not chained down
but Allesandro isn't convinced
we'll be able to carry even one out
unnoticed.

XVI
It smells like poetry in here.

XVII
A robot cleans the wheels.

XVIII
I try to convince everyone
you could disguise these as
car wheels and drive away.

XIX
My first book was called
Paris: It's the Cheese.
I may call this one
Italy: It's Also the Cheese.

Between Cheese and Balsamic

I
We leave the cheese behind
but the scent in the aging room
will stay with me for as long
as my nose is connected
to my brain.

II
A bear will serve you candy from its tray
is what another caution sign tells me.

III
Reggio Emilia is strategically located
near airports and Milan and the ocean
and as close as possible to *quiet*.

Balsamic - Aceto Balsamico Cavalli

I
In the winter nothing happens
because the temperature isn't right.

II
PDO is better than PGI.
Every step must be produced in this area.
With PGI, only one step. With PGI stuff could
come from anywhere.

III
The angels take a share
of the balsamic too.

IV
In the smallest barrel
of the line of six, which
contains some from all
other barrels, after twelve
years, it's a possibility
it might be considered
balsamic.

V
The oldest balsamic is black.

VI
The first taste
just the wine
is sweet like
Manischewitz.

VII
The second
vinegar makes
my face implode.

VIII
We're going to make our fortune
selling barrels of balsamic!

IX
Each new generation gets their
own barrel and they are passed from
generation to generation.

X
1000 years ago (1046)
the king of Germany
wanted some of this vinegar.

XI
Mrs. Cavalli, *Luisa*,
told us everything.
She comes from
farther than lake Como,
near the border
of Switzerland.

Between Balsamic and Wine

I
A deer will leap over your car
to impress the other deer
is what another caution sign
tells me.

II
The road will crumble
underneath your car
says yet another
caution sign.

Wine — Bertolani

I
The second fermentation
is when the bubbles come.

II
I assure him *nitrogen* is a word
but the Italians just aren't sure
it's the right one.

III
Addie gets the Italian test warning
on her phone five minutes after the rest of us.

IV
It's a family winery —
When you die, you get a wine
named after you.

Fred and Vincent
      both have a wine
Andre
      isn't ready yet.
Giancarlo
      just died and doesn't have one yet
Vincent and Alfredo
      are remembered on bottles.

V
We could make our fortune
selling fermented bottles of
Vincent wine.

VI
It takes a week to slowly rotate
the wine bottles to allow the
sediment to collect at the opening
before it is removed.

VII
It's a new building but the wood door
to the aging room was made by
Vincent from the ancient winery.

VIII
I ask if Andrea will open
a 1959 bottle for us.
The quick answer is *no*.

IX
If the wine is sweet
you can hide the problems.

X
Every winery makes a choice.

XI
Try Bertolani's
Rossi All'antica.
I insist.

XII
Every label has a story.
The *Rabesco* has an engraving from
Andrea's grandfather's sister.
She's 99 today.

XIII
After all the wine
I'm able to say
It's so nice.
My butt hurts.

Between Wine and Reggio Emilia

We drive by a restaurant
called *Little Italy*.
Wait a minute …

In Reggio Emilia

I
In San Prospero Square
an artisan gently pounds
bricks into the square floor
to complete it for future feet.

II
The restaurant sign says
Pizza and Food which
makes me wonder
what pizza is.

III
Sitting with Addie in the gelato shop —
music at level 11 starts out of the speakers
and eventually goes down to a listenable amount.

A woman apologizes in Italian.
I will not be hiring her to
operate my stereo.

IV
We walk by a building
made in 1186. America
wasn't even sucking
at King George's teat yet.

V
The afternoon siesta
which probably is a
different word here
made it seem like
no one lives, eats,
or works in Reggio Emilia.

Train Back

I
The train back to Bologna is also six stops.
Please read the poem which begins on page 82
backwards for the full experience.

II
A man somehow gets ahead of Addie
on the way to the seats (she's a much
less aggressive walker than me)
and almost becomes my new wife
as he tries to take the seat next to me.
I point to Addie which in any language
means *this seat is not for you.*

III
Addie's elbow touches mine and
she explains she's just *airing out*
and that she also might be a chicken.

IV
I simultaneously never want to eat again
while making a dinner reservation.

V
*Please run in the train
in that direction* is what,
I'm sure, one sign is indicating.

VI
I have the status of this train
on my phone so I don't need to
stretch to see the sign.
Come to think of it
I have the status of
everything everywhere
on my phone.

VII
In the middle of being a chicken
Addie says *no* to being a chicken
and then continues being a chicken.
She still refuses to peck for food though.
(That's right, *still*.)

VIII
A man walks up the middle
with a white wash-cloth, like he's
the Pavarotti of this train.

IX
Graffiti is weird here —
a drawing of Terrance and Phillip.
The word *Ikea*.
Donut misspelled.

The Six Problems With Dinner

I
A dog peed on the amplifier
of the man playing guitar
near our outside table.

II
They brought us the wrong dish and we
didn't realize which prevented us from
getting out of Bologna, without actually
eating any bologna.

III
The fried potatoes dish
turned out to be potato chips.
House-made, so, cool I guess
but not what we'd hoped for.

IV
A German man sat at the awkward
end space of the long table next to us
causing him to invade my air space
for all of the meal.

V
The *Tide to Go* stick didn't make it
into the evening bag so when one
of my tortelloni fell off my fork and
onto the plate, it splashed butter
onto my white shirt in six places
with no reasonable plan to deal
with it at all.

VI
The Water Incident —
Addie choked a little on water
as I was writing down the first
set of problems, and held up
a certain number of fingers
indicating there was an
additional problem.

Conversation, Also at the Restaurant

Your spoon is bigger.
Because I'm a man.
This is my man spoon.

De Niro

Tonight's movie in Piazza Maggiore
is *Casino*. I don't think I've heard
the word *fuck* broadcast so loudly
to so many people in an
outdoor space before.

Goodnight Bologna

We came to Italy for the food
and Bologna did not disappoint.
Our stomachs have contacted
contractors for the needed expansion.
I don't know who's going to pay for that
but I do know this famous city, hardly
on any tourist's radar, should be on
every tourist's radar. Its piazzas
are alive like the ones we remember
in Rome nineteen years ago.
It's Apérol Spritzes do the job!
We barely touched a museum here
but that's okay! Your tortelloni
and cheese and Lambrusco
told us almost everything we
needed to know. Plus, when
you're walking through a living museum
it has to count for something.
We saw at least five of your seven secrets.
(I'll never tell.) We stood on your
tallest tower. Oh, Bologna,
tomorrow morning will be bittersweet.
Should I do another double espresso
or maybe a cappuccino this time?
You tell me what I should do.
Even after I leave, you know
how to get in touch. I'll follow
whatever instructions you send my way.

A Day in Which We Leave Bologna

and go to Florence

Carrot Muffin

At breakfast this morning
Addie said the word *carrot*
to me and it took me a while
to determine she was assessing
my muffin and wanted me to
confirm or deny.

I wasn't sure but it said the word
carrot on the wrapper so
it's a probability.

I'm probably going to
change my shirt, that is
put on a different one
for reasons I'd rather not
get into but I didn't want
to leave you completely
out of the loop.

Who are you anyway?
Send an email with all the details.

It's our last few feet
on the Bologna ground
before the all-too-short
train to Florence.

Whoever you are
whatever shirt you
are wearing.
I will surely
keep you up to date
on whatever is next.

Fortune

The inside of my
now empty espresso cup
is being coy with me
about the day.

Our Bologna Breakfast Guy

Our guy isn't at breakfast
so God knows who our tip
will be going to. He was *our* guy.
Prided himself on remembering
our coffee orders and brought
out the gluten-free basket without
being asked. I guess today
is his day off. He deserves it
our guy. Our Bologna breakfast guy.

At the Clock Tower

We visit the *Torre dell'Orologio*
after which our hotel was named.
Its building began in 1249.
A fire melted the bell in 1492
Cheerful fireworks they called it.
The current clock — from 1774.

This giant clock face
tells me it is ten minutes
after Italian o'clock.

Turns out the building holes
were for scaffolding necessary
to make the buildings.

I'd like to apply for the job
of *clock keeper.* I'd be honest
not like the guy they had to fire.

I can see all of Bologna
from the clock tower.
There's so much of Bologna
I have yet to see.

It's not quite stairs.
It's not quite a ramp —
the way down from the second floor.
Addie does an interpretive
dance appropriate to this situation.

I sit in one of the chairs
in the senate room and
begin my barrage of *nos*
to anything anyone says.

What She's Going Through

Addie's hair has not been sitting
where she wants. It's true.
I saw it in a chair in a
completely different piazza.

We're Leaving Bologna

I
The Piazza Maggiere
may never touch these sneakers again.
Neptune. You are mine.
Always.

II
Now we are the people walking down
Via d'ell'Indipendenza, rolling our luggage
towards the train station. Nobody wants this.

III
The Garibaldi statue of him on a horse
on Via d'ell'Indipendenza is not Roy Rogers,
no matter what anyone tells you.

IV
The word for *phone case* in Italian is *carcass*
which makes me think of all the times my phone
almost fell off the tallest tower in Bologna,
leaving a carcass of its former self
on the Bologna ground.

P.S. Upon researching this back at home I've learned
this is not correct and I have no idea what that sign
we walked by in Bologna was advertising.

V
Florence is only a thirty-seven minute ride
from Bologna. Are we even going anywhere?

On the Train

The *in-roll* magazine
is in Italian.

I am rolling backwards
Addie is rolling forwards.
This is what I want for her.
Plus my view is her eyes.

Finally, someone checks our tickets.
We could have rolled for free
all over Emilia-Romagna.

We emerge from a tunnel and
I can finally see...never mind
we just went into another tunnel.

I think we're going under
the mountains between
Emilia-Romagna and Tuscany.
But then again I think
a lot of things.

I can buy products
on this train *for every moment
of my day.*

Finally, we emerge from the tunnels and
nope another tunnel.

On the screen, a cartoon —
a baby jumps on the back of a robot
who kicks a soccer ball
annoying a squirrel.
Then the robot's feet turn into nets
and they fly around the world.
Cut back to the original room
with baby and robot holding
a little Eiffel Tower.

Finally, we emerge from the tunnels.
The graffiti of the outskirts of Florence
is present. *Bongo Pitts* is painted on one wall.
There's a fancy robot too.
Florence, we are arriving.

Walk to the Hotel

I
Where are the porticos of Bologna
I cry as we walk in the hot sun towards
our Florence hotel.

II
I see our first *David's* penis on an apron
at a small stand near the train station.
We'll see the real thing soon enough.

III
I feel sad for the people walking with their luggage
towards the train station, knowing they're feeling
what I just felt in Bologna. I hope their experience
was as good as ours will be.

Quiet Mime!

After the best sandwich
we've ever had in Florence

(and also the only sandwich
we've ever had in Florence)

in front of the longest sandwich line
we've ever seen in any city

at another sandwich shop
we see a talking mime.

We're not sure if he's off duty,
or just isn't very good.

Quacking by Ponte Vecchio

Addie starts to quack.
I don't turn around because
I am headed to a particular picture spot.
She quacks even more vigorously
trying to get my attention. She's upset
that I don't turn around, but I just assumed
this is when Addie quacks in Florence
and it's a normal thing.

Overheard

We overhear a woman tell another woman *I'll meet you over there because I have to go to the other product.* This is at least a *two product* kind of town.

Florence Free Walking Tour

I
First of all the tour guide
didn't have the promised
blue umbrella, so God knows
who's about to walk us around Florence.

II
Our guide is Daniel instead of *Donato*
as was promised in the confirmation email.
It's probably fine.

III
Michelangelo worked
at *this church* when he
was a teenager.

IV
Now we are entering
the *old city* that the
Romans made.

V
We stop by the window
of *beautiful women*.
They let Addie right in.

VI
We see ancient horse parking spots.

VII
Wine doors from the time of the plague
were used again when COVID came along.

VIII
When rich people wanted to make a new building
they had to make a stone bench all around it
so poor people could sit.

IX
You can walk on the *Via Roma*
all the way to Rome. It's not that complicated.
This is one of the *all roads* that lead there.

X
Remind me not to remove the lantern
from the top of the Duomo when we
go up there as everything will fall down.

XI
The Medici house was the first renaissance building
in Florence. Everyone rich copied them after.

XII
The big ball
on top of the Duomo
is very big.

XIII
The green white and red colors of the Duomo
has nothing to do with the same colors of the Italian flag.

XIV
A tower from six hundred and nine years after Christ
became a jail, became storage for merchants,
became expensive apartments.

XV
No tower could be taller than Castle Vecchio.

XVI
The reason for lanterns was because
it was *super dark*.

XVII
Here's a naked guy statue.
Now, every time I see one of these
I check the floor for a secret dick viewing stone.

XVIII
One bad guy who defeated the Medicis
burned all the philosophy books
and passed a law saying women could
only wear black, white, and gold as
all other colors were distracting from God.

XIX
Amerigo Vespucci
named almost all the countries
in all the Americas.

XX
The Ponte Vecchio — *the old bridge* —
was made by the Romans.
The Medici's secret passage runs on top of it.

XXI
The bridge used to house butcheries and fish markets.
Now it's expensive shops. The Medicis kicked out the
fisher-people and butchers because it smelled.

XXII
Tourists cannot go in the secret passage
but they are trying to fix the problem.

XXIII
The German commander didn't bomb
the Ponte Vecchio when they were retreating
from the allies (from Rome) because
he loved the bridge too much.

XXIV
There's a lot of competition amongst the
gel-ball-throwing guys on the bridge.
(Unless they're in it together.)

XXV
The jewelry shops on Ponte Vecchio
need to rebuild their multi-paneled
wooden doors when they close.

XXVI
I'm feeling a little guilty about
telling everyone about
the secret passage.

XXVII
Gian Gastone was the last ruler
of the Medici family.
Inbreeding and gout led to no children.
All of them were gone by 1743.

XXVIII
Gelato was invented for the wedding of
Katherine de Medici.

XXIX
Bontalenti.
He invented gelato.
We're going to eat it.

XXX
The two-hour free tour ended early.
I'm not sure if I got my money's worth.

We're on Our Own Now

Addie quacks to make sure
I see the fluffy dog ahead as
I was buried in my phone
writing the last thing.

At Osteria Filetto d'Oro

I
Our server's name is *David*.
After the statue I ask?
Yea, he's my dad, he answers.

II
In this heat and and in this not air-conditioned dining room
I don't feel guilty about wearing a t-shirt
I bought at the Magic Kingdom.

III
Conversation in the restaurant:
I make this wine.
You personally make this wine?
No.

IV
How many glasses in a bottle, Addie asks.
I've never seen a glass in a bottle
I triumphantly answer.

V
Florence has lots of places to get kebob.
If you want a *kebap* you have to go to
Reggio Emilia.

VI
I want to go to the table where the young
American kids are yelling *Uno* at each other
and speak in an accent of some kind and
tell them *this is not how we behave in
restaurants in Italy.*

Now the young girl is twerking at her family.
*We do not twerk in Italia, little girl, maybe Naples
but definitely not Florence,* I tell her in
my fantasy accent.

VII
If they offer Limoncello
you have to say *yes*.
It's a *Super Size Me* thing.

VIII
David, our waiter, noticed my cat photo
on my phone and wants to show us his dog.
A pit bull. He's a happy dog.

Secrets

I
We found a secret dick on a statue in Piazza della Signoria.

II
Speaking of secrets, Addie thinks the secret walkway would be more secret if it were underground instead of visible to everyone.

Turns Out Florence Is Pretty Good

I have to admit when we walked out of
the train station in Florence, the immediate
neighborhood didn't give me hope.

But then we entered the old city and
in front of me was the Duomo and one of
the largest churches in the world.

I got the Florence feels right away.
Lunch and a walking tour later and
I knew we were going to be alright.

I'm trying not to tell Jude at camp in
my nightly messages too much about
the pasta here because he's already

upset that he didn't get to come and
pasta, historically, is his favorite food.
But I think I can tell you, we've

eaten some historic pasta here.
It is *all the degrees* here and I'm not
sure if I'm gaining weight because

I'm eating so much, or losing weight
because I'm sweating so much.
I asked Jude to let me know what I

look like when I see him again.
There's a lot to do before that happens.
I miss Bologna, but some of the most

famous things artists ever created
are about to be in my eyes. We also
saw a long line for sandwiches and

although one of us is indifferent
about sandwiches, we LOVE a good line.
We're living like there's no tomorrow

and eagerly planning tomorrow.
I'm writing this at the end of your workday
and at the end of my whole day.

I'll see you tomorrow.

Florence Day One

I have nothing to add to this section title

At Breakfast

I
Addie's tongue knew
just where to go to
capture the small bit
of cappuccino foam
from just above her lip
without missing
a moment of
eye contact.

II
Then she takes her knife
and scoops a little of
my donut custard
to use for her needs.

Addie Becomes a Toad This Morning

When I point this out
she goes all in and, between laughs,
practices fly-grabbing.

The empty coffee mug
tells me *your wife will
become a toad.*

Addie suggests it's usually
the other way around.
You find a toad (kiss it)
and it becomes your wife.

We're still learning how
it works here.

Chairity

Addie spots a couple of chairs
in the breakfast room she'd like to
have for our living room at home.

She wonders if I can fit them in my bag.
To be clear, this is completely separate
from our Bologna plan to make our fortune
selling free-range stackable chairs.

Acknowledgment

We're off to see some of
the most famous paintings
in the world. *This world* ...
I think to myself, ominously.

Showtime

One of the American girls
at the table to my left
(Addie's right) is the
captain of the soccer team.
We've got a real live
Yellowjackets situation
in here.

At the Uffizi

I
Leda of the "Naples-uffizi type"
330-300 BCE

Hello
Topless
Duck
Lady

II
Group of Hercules Slaying the Centaur Nessus

Glad we walked down to the end of the gallery
to see the naked guy fighting the centaur.

III
Nymph with a Panther
2nd century BCE

How come the nymphs get all the Panthers
and I can't even have one?

IV
Madonna and Child
Ambriogi Lorenzetti 1329-1348

No one looks happy.
Not even the baby.

V
And the Jesus phase of our vacation has begun.

VI
The Redeemer Blessing
Spinello Aretino, 1383-5

This one is missing.
I guess someone is
making their fortune,
already, with Uffizi paintings.

VII
Madonna and Child Enthroned
Giotto di Bondone, 1306-10

Jesus was a fat baby.
Then again, so was ours.
Those chubs!

VIII
Mr. sticky-armed man
touches my elbow.
I don't like it.

IX
Addie agrees to find
the most important
painting in every room.

X
Glorification of the Angels and Saints
Fra Giovanni da Fiesole, 1434-5

Everybody gets a halo.

XI
Duke and Duchess of Urbino
Piera Della Francesca

The diptych couple loved each other
but still maintained separate paintings.
She has a big forehead.
He has a big hat.

XII
St. Vincent, St. James and St. Eustace
Antonio Del Pollaiolo, Circa 1496

St. James is secretly George Harrison.

XIII
We take a selfie in front of Botticelli's *Spring*.

XIV
Birth of Venus
Botticelli

She was born an adult
and immediately gets to
ride on a clamshell.

XV
A website man says after seeing this painting
he left a life of Wall Street banking to become a tour guide.
I'm not sure the Medicis would've approved, but I do.

XVI
Adoration of the Shepherds with Angels and St. Thomas,
St. Anthony the Abbot, St Margaret, St. Mary Magdalene
and the Portinari family; Annunciation
Hugo van der Goes, 1440-82

One of the Marx brothers appears in this one.
I'm not sure which one. The two-headed child
is the main focus.

XVII
It's raining tits in the map room.

XVIII
Medici Venus in the Tribuna

You can't even go in the room.
See her from a distance.
We see her from all angles
thanks to our patience.

She's got it.

XIX
Christ continues in the next gallery.

XX
Lamentation over the Body of Christ
Giovanni Bellini, 1500-06

Black and white Jesus.
Bellini gets a drink
named after him.

XXI
Portrait of a Lady
Veneto o Lombardia, 1520-30

Put your arms down lady. It's not the painter's fault.

XXII
St. Sebastian
Ambito di Ercole de'Roberti, 1480-90

He looks a bit sassy for a guy impaled to a tree.

XXIII
Some of the sculptors were a
little loosy goosy with the butts.
Maybe they thought no one
would look at the behinds.

XXIV
Perseus Freeing Andromeda
Piero di Cosimo, 1510-15

...was a party.

XXV
Addie counts all the babies in room 32.

XXVI
You may not be aware of this —
Leonardo da Vinci made
more than one painting.

XXVII
Holy Family with the Young St. John the Baptist, "Doni Tondo"
Michelangelo Buonarroti, 1505-07

We finally found the round painting we've been told to look for.

XXVIII
My historical study of statues and paintings
tells me they didn't invent clothing until 1583.

XXIX
The Vision of St. Bernard
Fra' Bartolomeo, 1504-1507

You either get a halo or wings, but not both.

XXX
Statue Observations

The first ultimate frisbee game.
Pompeii just before the lava came.
Want to buy a pen?
Adolfo, I'm over here.
I want to suck your blood.
Wow put that thing away.
I am the wind.
Testify!

XXXI
For a brief moment,
Addie wasn't sure
what to do with her face,
so she did everything
with her face.

XXXII
Group of Pan and Daphne
Greek Marble 2nd-1st Century BCE

If you want Pan to teach you how to play flute,
you're gonna have to be naked.

XXXIII
14. Hermaphrodite
Roman art, 1st century

The hermaphrodite gets their own room.
Demands a certain privacy.

XXXIV
Portrait of Man
Hans Memling, 1890

Addie's been looking for this hair the whole time.
The Afro of its day.

XXXV
From a window —
The rooftops of Florence
Ancient tiles
LG air-conditioners
Terra cotta
TV Antenna
The sky doesn't care.

XXXVI
We enter the self-portraits floor.
My eyes in the bathroom a minute ago
showed me I look like Cosmo Kramer.

XXXVII
Selfies took a lot longer
when the only way to do it was
to paint yourself.

XXXVIII
Autoritratto
Jean-Étienne Liotard, 1744

Mr. Fancy Man
with his Russian hat —
I'm not even sure the Russians
were a thing in 1744.

XXXIX
Addie says *I'll paint you
if you paint me.*
There's no one I'd rather
still life with than you, Addie.

XL
Every painting
was modern art
the day it was painted.

XLI
Raimondo Zaballi
Circa 1842

Yes. If I were a painter
mostly I'd be painting cats too.

XLII
The weird body-contorting dance
you do when you realize you're standing
in front of a stranger's camera.

XLIII
Living: Some Days...
Jenny Holzer, 1982

*"Some days you wake up and
immediately start to worry.
Nothing in particular is wrong.
It's just the suspicion that
forces are aligning quietly
and there will be trouble."*

XLIV
Judith with the Head of Holofernes
Jacopo Negretti, 1525-1528

Girl's gotta eat.

XLV
Venus, Known as the "Venus of Urbino"
Tiziano Vecellio, 1538

Okay but mainly I'm interested in the puppy.

XLVI
Testa di Medusa
Caravaggio, 1597

They say Caravaggio's paintings
made people uncomfortable.
When my butt, behind the Medusa,
made the alarm go off
I got uncomfortable.

After the Uffizi

We have just seen some of the most famous paintings on this Earth. My eyes will never be the same.

Comfort

By law they build stone benches around
the exterior of Florence houses so the poor
will have a comfortable place to be.
In Los Angeles they put bumps
in the benches so no one there
can be comfortable.

More Than a Fly

Addie wants to know if I want to
be in a room with Phil Rosenthal
and what I would say to him.
I do and I don't know I tell her
and she says she is willing to be
more than a fly in that room which
I hope makes as much sense to you
as it does to me.

At the Accademia Gallery

I
Everyone who has ever existed
is wandering the streets of Florence.
Every one of them is trying to see the
statue of *David* today.

Couldn't some of you have come tomorrow?

II
The Rape of the Sabines
Jean de Boulogne, 1579-1583

A statue in the middle
not located in Christ Corner.

One could argue it is a more
compelling work of art than *David*.

III
The hall of prisoners is filled with
unfinished Michelangelos.
and leads to *David*
who is finished.

IV
The unfinished ones were
because of budget cuts
and an eventually dead Pope.

V
Michelangelo simply
removed all the stone
that wasn't David who
was trapped inside.

VI
The announcement to *be silent*
is the loudest thing I've ever heard.

VII
We have learned the word *polyptych* today.

VIII
In the *Hall of Busts* I think
we could make our fortune selling busts,
I could sneak them out and tell them
no, no these are my heads.

IX
Mr. Holy Faced Man
and his lifelong companion
Mrs. Holy Face.

(Just down the way are their holy faced children.)

X
Bacchae With a Woman, a Faun and a Panther
Francesco Pozzi. 1789-1844

This was always my vision for Addie and Jude.

XI
Well, I guess several hundred heads
are better than one.

XII
I'd like to buy a life-sized *David* statue
and put it in Jude's room but everything
is wrong with that idea.

XIII
We climb many stairs to the top floor
only to find a single gallery with
a lot more Christ Polyptychs.

XIV
I think a single panel painting
is called a *painting*.

XV
Addie bonds with a woman we saw
on our tour yesterday, not only over
their outfits, but when she asks if
they'd walked behind *David*
all of their eyes lit up after the
word *behind*.

XVI
The cash register lady was also
endeared with Addie when she
presented the *David's* butt postcard
to purchase.

Porno for Pyros

When Porno for Pyros announced
tickets going on sale for their
first tour in three decades
I spend time in the hotel
reserving my tickets.

Face Off

After dinner I tell Addie
I'm going to go wipe off my face
which she doesn't find as alarming
as I think she should.

The Limoncello Rule

The rule is still if we are offered
a Limoncello we must say *yes*.
They did not offer us a Limoncello
at the vegetarian restaurant we
were at tonight, which was only
one of the disappointing things
about that place. So I offered
Addie a Limoncello at a much nicer
place we happened to walk by
and she was obligated to say *yes*.

Florence Day Two

in which we spend a second day in Florence

Good Morning, Florence

It is difficult to know what day it is on a trip like this.
Often, extra time and thought has to go into determining

this information when someone (like your wife)
asks you *what day is it*, or you need a reference

for when you are scheduled to be somewhere
or leave a city.

This morning the double espresso is
not quite as strong as the other days

and we are going to visit all the
Catholicism possible. We are going to

climb up the Catholicism and see what
we can see from the top of the Catholicism.

We're hoping not to fall off the Catholicism.
We have to wear special clothes to

not offend the Catholicism and we will
go into the museum of Catholicism.

I'm also hoping for a gift shop of Catholicism.
They have the biggest Catholicism here

and we hope to be impressed by it
despite our different allegiances and

regardless of what day it is.
We've got Judaism scheduled for later.

They have just a little bit of Judaism here.
I just wish today's (It could be Thursday.

How do you even know?) coffee was
so much stronger.

Inside Voices

Addie says we're going to have to
practice our *inside voices* for the church.
I'm hoping they have a person sitting
in a chair whose exclusive job is to,
every three minutes, whisper
shhhhhhh as loud as possible.

Weather Report From Addie

There will be a zero percent chance of rain.
She clarifies: *There will be a fifty percent chance of zero inches of rain.*

I'm selling my empty breakfast plates
for umbrellas that weigh nothing.

Americans Gone Wild

A young girl argues
with her young brother

about whose responsibility
it is to *do the keycard*.

She insists it is her job.
She has already pushed

two tables together for her family
who had already set up shop

at a different set of tables.
She did a good job for another family.

The breakfast she has chosen is
a festival of desserts and someone else's

children would be jealous or proud
and her parents don't say a thing.

Too Late

I forgot to write a *Good Night Florence* poem
last night. I assure you the night ended
and it was good.

The Empire Is Mine

I
I found a secret doorway at the hotel
that goes all the way back to Julius Caesar.

II
I don't speak much Italian so odds are
this sign is not translated to
Creative Talking Fish.

III
Give me wine from a hole
or give me death!

IV
Now Addie is telling me
to use my *inside voice*
a whole lot more than
she ever did before.

The line to get into the cathedral is as long as the entirety of human civilization.

The
line
to
get
into
the
cathedral
is
as
long
as
the
entirety
of
human
civilization.

The Wine Hole Dilemma

During the plague, many restaurants,
instead of doors, created small holes
to provide food and drink to people
and allow for minimal contact.

These remained closed for centuries
until COVID when some of them
reopened and now, as a curiosity
you can order wine from some of them.

All of this is to say, Jay, considering
your disparate feelings about wine
and holes, would you get wine from
a wine hole?

In the Duomo

I
This is the cathedral that stood
without a dome for a hundred years
until technology caught up with
the need for a roof.

II
Pigeons don't need tickets.

III
Person walking along
talking to himself —
with AirPods: *normal*
without: *crazy.*

IV
The other horses are jealous of the one
with its feed bag attached to its neck.
That horse will take its hay to go.

V
Across from the cathedral entrance is
Mister Pizza. Previously I'd wonder
if there was a *Mrs. Pizza,* but now I just
want to know what it's pepperonouns are.

VI
You climb the dome and the bell tower here.
Addie has agreed to one climbing and
if I need to climb something else we can
come back another day.

VII
One guy from a website says there are
eighty-two vendors selling scarves
you can purchase in case you have
shown up with visible shoulders.

VIII
Addie leaves the line momentarily
to visit the leather shop across the way.
It's going to be a hell of an evening.

IX
They funnel a certain number of
people directly into the empty graves
in the crypt for crowd control and efficiency.

X
A panther and a lion
welcome us into the cathedral.

XI
I say some particularly hilarious things.
Addie responds with a practiced silence
appropriate for whenever I open my
big mouth.

XII
Inside the cathedral —
another opportunity to
make our fortune selling chairs
presents itself.

XIII
I would, a hundred percent,
rearrange the chairs before
leading services in this space.

XIV
We see a skull in a gated room —
a warning to me and whatever
I might be considering.

XV
Parts of a belt buckle from a tomb
on display can only mean the
dead guy's pants have fallen down.

XVI
We climb down into the crypt.
As much as I like climbing up something,
climbing down something is
a close second.

XVII
The climb up the Dome
may have fifty or so fewer steps
than the tower we climbed in Bologna,
so I'll be incrementally closer to
not having a heart attack.

XVIII
All I know is I'm not
carrying that baby
all the way up the Duomo.

XIX
Wondering if they'll let me walk up topless
to avoid the shirt sweats. Or, do I take off my shirt
halfway up, after we're through security
and the Italian Catholic shirt police.

XX
Addie puts her hand in a hole.
Out of holbit.

P.S. *Holbit,* pronounced hole-bit,
is now a real word, but don't look it up
as you're reading this too soon and they
haven't had a chance to add it to where
they keep all the words.

XXI
narrow passageway
in between two domes

XXII
Either the employees have to
climb up this every day, or one
of the benefits of employment
is airlifting.

XXIII
I notice a lot of good Duomo holes.
Each hole is better than the last.

XXIV
What secrets are buried
under these stones?

The kind only discovered by
legends described in

ancient texts in even
older languages.

What treasures and magic
have yet to see oxygen

for over
two thousand years?

In the Opera del Duomo Museum

I
Gates of Paradise Bapistery Doors
Lorenzo Ghiberti, 1401-1422

The twenty feet tall, eight feet wide, ornately decorated
with three dimensional gold carvings Bapistery Doors
make me feel like we've got to up our door game
back in Newhall.

II
Addie points out all the headless statues
in the model of the medieval facade
and I remind her they didn't invent heads
until 1478.

III
God Creating Eve
Andrea Pisano, 1334-1343

God pulls Eve out of Adam
fully formed, except the missing arm.
Adam sleeps through
the whole procedure.

IV
Daedalus: The Mechanical Arts
Andrea Pisano, 1348-50

A cross between
Aquaman, Hawkman
and Chris Hemsworth.

V
Hercules and Cacus
Andrea Pisano, 1348-50

Hercules lost half his leg.
Powers through it.

VI
Donato (or Priscian): Grammar
Luca della Robbia, 1437-1439

Half of student's face is stuck in the wall.
Like a game of *Portal* gone bad.

VII
Orpheus: Music
Luca della Robbia, 1437-1439

I see Orpheus from *Hadestown*.
Or maybe he was here first.

VIII
Statue of a Beardless Prophet
Donatello, 1415-1418

Labeled *beardless*, we learn the statue
didn't grow a beard until 1419.

IX
Cantoria
Luca della Robbia, 1431

It takes a lot longer to get through
Psalm 150 if you're carving each line
as a complicated relief into stone
instead of singing it.

X
All of these ancient beautiful things
were decorations in the original cathedral.
We never would have been able to see them
this close if it weren't for a flood in the sixties.

XI
The *modern art* is from the eighteen hundreds.
Adam and Eve look humble.
They know what they did.

XII
We're tired but the sign that says
Fragments of Magnificence
is compelling.

XIII
Pietà
Michelangelo, 1547-1555

His next to last sculpture.
He almost destroyed it.

XIV
Miniature statues of *David* cost
different amounts everywhere
so don't rush to buy the first one
you see unless that's the least expensive,
in which case go back and get it,
unless you don't want one
in which case don't bother reading this.

XV
Michelangelo carved *David* in this space
where Brunelleschi had his offices while
building the Duomo. Now we pass through
these doors of history for more of this place
of *everything*.

All'Antico Vinaio

I
I've got sandwich all over my face.

II
I am eating the sandwich of my ancestors.
At least the 1% of them who were Italian
according to the DNA test.

III
Where once there was a sandwich
now there is none.

At Santa Croce

I
Some tombs have no names —
just symbols or family crests.
They were important enough to be buried here
but still somehow anonymous.

II
Galileo's head and the rest of his body
are in three blocks — his triumphs were
looking up the truth.

III
The statue on top of A.G.B. Niccolini's tomb
looks like the Statue of Liberty.

IV
Michelangelo
who is in this box
who made the *David* —
did he make the statues
which adorn his tomb?

V
A small child who may not know better
dances in front of Michelangelo's tomb.

VI
Who are these people
buried at his feet?

Who are these people
who I am standing on
while writing this?

VII
I see an empty space
where they could put
my box.

VIII
On second thought
bury me at Michelangelo's feet
but leave a space for Addie
and don't let her use it
for a thousand years.

IX
I see the small chapel
where we will lead Shabbat
after angling the benches
of course.

X
I could confess in this building
with the facilities they provided.
But I'm not going to.

We walk by a second Mister Pizza.

I realize it may be a polyamory thing.

The Jewish Synagogue and Museum

After a day full of churches we stopped by
The Jewish Synagogue and Museum which
featured more stairs, and artifacts which were

familiar to us because of the things we do.
I said *shalom* to everyone there and, maybe
it was the heat, but none of them seemed

interested. *Italian before Jewish* one video
told us in which the people were indifferent
about the synagogue after it was built.

We feel both at home and *indifferented*.
It took lot of money to make this building and
most of it came from David Levi who died before

they even started to build it. It takes a lot of
faith to pay for a future you will not see.
Thank you, David, for we got to see what you

wanted us to see. Just to keep you up to date
our people have still not discovered air-conditioning
at least not in Italy. Still, it's nice to know we have

a home in a place that is not our home. At least
not today. Who knows what the future holds.
I'm one percent Italian. This could be it.

Stop

There are *stop* signs
and they're in English
which may be why
people are only
vaguely stopping.

To Hell With Florida

From our hotel window I can see the top of the Duomo
where we stood earlier today after climbing many steps.

There are people standing where we stood. I can see them
but, in my current state of dress, I'm hoping they

cannot see me. Not that I am moving further away from
the window. This is Italy. This is Florence. Home of

Michelangelo, who made *David*, who people in Florida
are now trying to categorize as *pornography*.

My full *David* is on display at the window. Let the people
who did the work with their feet see what they may.

Song

Today, what I did
made Addie sing
Ave Maria.

(I may be giving myself
too much credit.)

At La Bottega di Via Maggie

I
The server tells us in person
he will arrive in a bit.

II
I've had *miniature horse* level
of drinks tonight and it's a miracle
that any of these words
are spelled correctly.

III
The waiter sits down with the people
at the other table. I think after this wine
and the Limoncello spritz earlier,
if we stay here long enough, Daniel,
our waiter, will be our best friend too.

IV
Daniel is the most Italian man
we've ever met. The way he speaks
adding extra vowels to the end of words.

It is not natural for an Italian to end a word
with a consonant. He has the most
Italian mustache too. We take photos

with Daniel. Not just because of the wine
but because he is a human being whose
Italian smile was the amuse bouche we needed.

When the flute player plays

Can't Help Falling in Love
on one side of the Ponte Santa Trinita,
I can't help wondering how he knows,
and why this song comes up
wherever we go.

Good Night Florence

Florence is an excessive city that never sleeps
at least not while we are out and about in it.

Maybe it's gone to sleep now that we've
gone back to our room. We've had all the

gelato and most of the pasta, and certainly
all the bread and cheese. I'm not sure there

is any wine or Limoncello left now that we've
been here for two days. Tomorrow we will

be in this spot but before then we will be
in other cities to see what they look like

and what they're willing to feed us. We will
pray the tower doesn't finally fall when we

take our turn going up it. We will spend
hours on a bus between all these things.

For heaven's sake, how will I get all my steps?
I've been so good putting my feet in front of

my other feet. It may still be possible.
The hotel has promised to give us breakfast

even though it is before when they normally
would give us breakfast. All you have to do

is ask and they will give you all the *of course*
you want before you lay your head down

and then pick it back up again.

Florence Day Three

in which we spend the day in the part of Tuscany that is not Florence

Good Morning Florence

A morning walk through Florence
to the train station to not get on a train.
They are hosing down everything and
the restaurant tables are not awake yet.
The city has that new day smell. I manage
to not drop my double espresso on the
ground or, more importantly, on my shirt
which is the first small triumph of the day.
A day, I hope, that will be filled with
triumphs of many sizes, culminating with,
or at least including, a cow licking me.

Bus to Siena

I
*It is better to have someone dead in your house
rather than someone from Pisa.*

II
The Arno River that runs through
Florence, also runs through Pisa
so we could have floated there
rather than ridden on this
crowded bus.

III
Our guide is essentially putting
the microphone in her mouth.
The sound it produces accentuates
the war between Florence and Siena
that she describes.

IV
The microphone is rebelling against
our guide which is a nice respite
from the distortion, but not so good
for hearing anything.

V
This bus has USB ports in the ceiling
which may be the least convenient place
to have decided to put them.

VI
We drive by a mile of sunflowers.

VII
She is coming by to ask everyone
their meal preferences. I plan to tell her
she is talking too loud into the microphone,
a cow must lick me, and we are vegetarian.

VIII
Addie tells me she doesn't know what color Jude is.
Don't you remember? It's only been a week.
But she is referring to the camp *Color Wars* photos
she is looking at, trying to spot him. In that case
I don't know what color he is either, but I hope he
can make up with the people of the other colors
when the day is done so a Pisa, Florence, Siena
situation doesn't develop.

IX
Addie wants to make sure we have time to shop
tomorrow morning. I choke on some water when
she tells me this and say *if I am alive tomorrow,
I'll see what we can do.* Her first thought is *morbid*
but quickly adds *I may have to shop on my own.*

X
Jude is green.

XI
I overhear numerous people,
further back in the bus, saying
where are we over and over.
Feels like those people are
having a crisis. I don't know
where I am and I'm fine with that.

XII
The Tuscan countryside!
The Tuscan countryside!
The Tuscan countryside!

XIII
We drive by a castle on a hillside.
No one says anything so all I
can tell you is it's a castle
on a hillside.

XIV
I understand that parts of our body
can go to sleep on their own, but
do they also have their own dreams?

XV
There's a nearby *Museum of Torture*
as best as I can tell.

Siena

I
The fortress built by the conquering Medicis
is only good for walking your dogs
our local guide tells us.

II
She shows us her family cheese
at the farmers market.

III
Catherine met the pope
and then she *naturally died*.
They dismembered her body
so they could bury her in both
Rome and Siena.

IV
She agrees to tell us her name —
Analisa.

V
The post office is the only
new building in the old city.
It was the internet of its day.

VI
This road connected France and Rome.
Can you imagine how many people
stopped in this spot to change money,
to eat chicken soup?

VII
We are the descendants of
the traveler.

VIII
She apologizes they
haven't picked up the trash yet.

IX
A seventeen-year-old girl with a pacifier —
she won the horse race and it's
like she was reborn.

X
We walk through the *Dragon*
then *Owl* districts.

XI
If we take a left here
in ten days we will
arrive in Rome.

XII
The main square is an *odd shape*
because no one planned it.

XIII
Here, for sure, the holes are for the birds.

XIV
The horse race takes one minute.
But the square is set up for a week
and takes another week to clean.

XV
We move from the *Forest* district
to the *Eagle* district.

The best district in town
is the *Seashell* district.

(Because it's where Analisa is from.)

XVI
It took two hundred years to build the cathedral.
Eight generations — no plan.

XVII
Michelangelo only made one of the fourteen statues
he was hired to make here. He left early and made *David*
a few months later. One is better than none.

XVIII
The Piccolomini family
produced two popes.
They were basically
a pope factory.

XIX
A room surrounded by
thick music books.
The *large print* editions.

XX
Addie points out the morning gelato hills.
Fresh and ready. Unlike the late night
gelato caverns we have tasted.

XXI
Addie wants to buy a carrot at the market
to compare to the ones back in Newhall.
Fortunately, there isn't time so I don't have
to worry about importing Sienese carrots
from now on.

XXII
Siena is famous for banking
so we grab one of Banca di Roma's
famous deposit slips and head
out of town with all our money.

XXIII
Barely a taste of Siena
or perhaps *mostly* a taste
as we were given *Panforte*
in one shop, and Napolese
chocolates and pistachio cookies
in another. The cathedral was
at least as beautiful as the one
in Florence and had a bonus
Michelangelo for us to enjoy
before meeting back in the
imperfect, unplanned square
to head off to lunch on a farm
and hopefully a cow and her tongue.

The Winery

I
We are driving under the Tuscan sun
to lunch at a winery and restaurant
to eat focaccia, pasta with tomato sauce
and a plate of cheese and vegetables.
We have come to Italy for the food
(and the cow). This is what we are doing.
This is why we are here.

II
Addie's beauty blends
into the countryside. You
can't tell them apart.

III
Now I'm afraid that I might not
get to meet a cow and am prematurely
composing a haiku about it.
(This is not that haiku.)

IV
Lots of bales of hay.
Even a small area in the middle
of a u-turn has grape vines.
Every patch is special.
Every one must be used.

V
Wheat ready for baling —
the loaves of bread of the future
spread out on Tuscan hills.

VI
It has been made clear to me
I will not be meeting a cow today.
I did get to see one down a hill
from about fifty yards away
as the crow flies, if crows flew
down hills. Our tour guide, Noemi,
promised to say *hello* to a cow for me
if she comes across one. Moo.

VII
I walk by Noemi again and say moo.
She promises to keep it in mind.

VIII
At Fattoria Poggio Alloro

We get four kinds of wine
plus bread and pasta and vegetables.

Even the eggplant is edible with this
Tuscan hills background.

A tractor goes by, as one would expect on a farm.
The whitest cows, just out of reach.

There is so much pleasantness to pour
in one's eyes. The first red wine is the best.

Though dipping cookies into the dessert wine
is something I would do again and again.

IX
Politics and time zones are discussed
at lunch amongst Australians, Californians
and two Cubans from Florida. No one
understands why anything has happened
the way it has happened.

X
At lunch the misters meant to
keep us cool don't work right.
Instead of being misted
we are irrigated.

XI
For sure a pointed email will be sent
to someone regarding the lack of
cow interaction.

XII
There goes another tractor.

XIII
All this wine —
I may sleep through
the climbing of Pisa.
Wake me when I'm
at the top.

San Gimignano

I
The towers here were
the first skyscrapers.

II
*Frolic across the street with
briefcase and small child*
a sign tells me.

III
They gave us wine and
set us loose in San Gimignano.
Where are your city cows,
oh San Gimignano?

IV
I ask Noemi if they have city cows.
She does not take me seriously.

V
A *tourist services offices* —
are cows considered a service?

VI
Overheard — *imagine a time when
we had to eat each other to death.*

VII
Two minutes into the old city
and we've already passed by
two museums of torture.

VIII
The gelato shop with the *best gelato in the world* sign
has a longish line. The other gelato shop, *Dondoli*,
whose sign only claims *the best gelato in Tuscany*
has a line leading all the way back to Rome.

IX
They say this is the *medieval Manhattan.*
But I say Manhattan is the modern San Gimignano.

X
A man in a red cleric robe recites what may be
the entire Bible in Latin. Though, I don't speak Latin
and it's also possible he is very dramatically reading
a script from a season one episode of *Friends*.

XI
The lemon gelato alone was worth
a stop in San Gimignano.

Pisa

I
The drive to Pisa is an hour and twenty minutes
and a good time for Noemi to, as she says, *shut up,
let us rest and view the many fields of sunflowers
we will pass.* Note taken, Noemi.

II
Pisa may be the last thing we go up during this trip.
We're halfway done and there are fewer things to go up.
We expect to still go *in* a lot of things. But less *up*.

III
I wonder if they weigh everyone
before letting them into the tower
just to be safe.

IV
All the sunflowers on the other side of the bus
are facing the bus, and the ones on our side
are facing away. First no cow, and now this.

V
The tower hasn't moved since 2008.
They say it should be safe for the next
two hundred years. This should be
enough time for our purposes.

VI
I think asking Noemi if there will
be a cow on top of the tower
may be going too far.

VII
We wait forever for a train
we're not even going to get on.

VIII
There's a public scale
on the walk to the tower
proving my theory.

IX
In the market on the road
towards the tower, one merchant's
entire sales pitch is *hello...something?*

X
I have the unique idea to
take a funny picture at the
Leaning Tower of Pisa.

XI
Heart zappers strategically located
at various levels up and down the tower.

XII
An old Italian woman tries to steal me
as her husband until she looks up and
realizes who I am not and immediately
gives up.

XIII
The most famous tower
was the easiest one to walk up
and I did ask for its autograph
though, as you may know,
old towers, or towers of any age,
are not able to sign things.

Back to Florence

I
We pass by watch towers
standing over a field of weeds.
Old prisoner of war camp?
What could have been there
and from when?

II
Was that a Roman aqueduct?
An old raised train track?
A structure built by genius dinosaurs?
Someone tell me something!

III
It's worth noting that Ferrari bought Fiat.
So if you buy a Fiat, you're essentially
buying a little Ferrari.

Ethnic

Korean, Indian, Bali —

we've arrived in
Little Everywhere Else.

Disposable

According to my device which
keeps track of things, I have achieved
500% of my *move goal*.

I never used to have a *move goal*
and now it's a habit which will,
hopefully, allow me to live forever.

I may be voiding the benefits of moving
by the amount of pasta I've put in me here.
When I get home, I'm going to

donate all my extra weight to charity.
The Australians we met today left without
saying *goodbye*. But the New Zealander

made an extra special point of it.
She carried around a disposable camera.
I hope she gets the prints before she

disposes of it. I don't remember
how those things work. *Better to dispose
of cameras than horde them*

I always say.

Goodnight Florence

We need a million more weeks
to see all of Florence, but instead
we just have this one last night.

I barely crossed the Arno three times.
I barely heard the name *Medici*
enough to picture their faces.

Michelangelo is an exception.
We saw him everywhere. He, and
his colleagues, carved this town

out of stones pulled from the ground.
The veins on *David*. The eyes on *Venus*,
the hole we never took wine from.

Let my feet touch this ground again
beyond tomorrow morning when
the train comes to take me to

where the lemons come from.

A Day Traveling to Naples

on an Italian train

The Lemon Song

Travel day and I am wearing
a t-shirt commensurate with this
situation. Allesandro, one of

our guys at the hotel, is still here
from last night! They work long
shifts here or perhaps they let

him sleep in an empty room.
At first he said it would not be
possible to drive us to Naples

in the event of a transportation
strike, but as we got to know him
better, he said he definitely would.

But only in the spirit that it was asked.
He knows our spirit now, so
anything is possible. Or at least

for the next couple of hours
until we wheel our bags down
the Florence streets to take

ourselves to the fully operational train
that will take us to Naples.
Napoli ... oh, Napoli.

Little Jars

Addie's yogurt
which came in a jar
which sealed the deal
is not sweetened and
not vanilla so is it
even anything?
It is when she
goes to get honey
which is also in
the littlest jar.

Everything!

I hope they have electricity
on the train because I would
like to plug in everything.
Everything!

Everything!

Big man comes
into the breakfast room
with a plate of everything.
Everything!

Everything Else!

One plate not enough
for big man. Goes to get
second plate filled
with everything else.
Everything else!

Not Good

Addie is hurting but
doesn't have a headache
which she describes as
Good. But not good.

Suggested postcard text for Addie's parents on the back of the "Borgo Sansepolcro 1410/1420-1492" painting postcard by Piero della Francesca.

Dear Mom and Dad,

It's Addie. Your daughter. I saw these two paintings and thought of you.

Love,
Addie Lupert

P.S. I have a different last name now.

A Lot!

Big man going to get a third plate!
It takes a lot to keep big man going.
A lot!

Far

Our boy has a headache
back in Simi Valley.
At least he still
has a head.

All of Humanity

The heat has communicated to us
that we will take a cab to the train station.

Now is the sad time our man Allesandro
tells us as we check out before his

colleague hails the cab.
Our driver takes us along the route

we just walked and now we see it
from the perspective of the cars

doing their best to not touch humans
in these narrow alleyways which

were never meant for them.
Are you allowed to run over a

minimum number of people, I ask him.
Does everyone get one a day?

He tells us there is a competition
and every day everyone loses.

The people are like lost sheep he tells us
as he narrowly avoids all of humanity.

Train to Napoli

I
Look at that boy.
He must be going to Naples.
Olive skin touched by the sea
rugged and thin. He must be
going to Naples. Unless
he's going to Rome.

II
Addie has discovered electricity on the train.
She's the Benjamin Franklin of the railway.

III
Addie is going backward
and may want to switch with me.
I am going forward and want
to go backward to when
all this began.

IV
Florence rolls away to my right.
Italy expands before my eyes.
Florence gets smaller and smaller
before Addie's.

V
So far I could walk
faster than this train.

VI
Graffiti of a steak
and then sunflowers.
Could also be
eggs gone bad.

VII
Now the train is moving
faster than I can walk.
This L.A. traffic we brought
with us can be so unpredictable.

VIII
They check our tickets and
I have once again passed the test
of knowing what I am doing.
(Especially if you ignore that
we sat in the wrong seats
when we got on the train.)

IX
I am eating train potato chips
and train cookies. I am drinking
train water. The train moisturizing
wipe leaves me sticky which,
I believe, goes against its
train mission.

X
I film forty-five seconds of
the Italian countryside.
It would have been a
minute but then one of
those pesky Italian tunnels
came along.

I wonder, when I
review this footage later
if I'll discover I've
inadvertently filmed
a murder. There's no
evidence so far of that
but the tunnel did
murder my view of
a field of sunflowers.

XI
This train ends in Naples
and then it becomes a train
that ends somewhere else.

XII
A dog somewhere between
Orvieto and Rome ignores
our train going by.

XIII
The Luperts have arrived in Rome!
But we don't get off the train so
the celebration is short lived.

XIV
I recommend to the tourists
exiting the train in Rome
make sure to look at all the old things
and eat lots of meals.
They are grateful for my insights.

XV
I hear a cat meowing somewhere
on this train, or just outside.
This sound has all my attention.

XVI
Instead of tourists on this leg
of the journey, it's loud Italian men
whose grandfathers fought in the war.

XVII
Leaving Rome it is now me
who is going backward.
I'll let you know when I
reach Caesar.

XVIII
Most people exited in Rome.
Maybe Addie and I will be the
only two people in Naples.

XIX
Thanks to electricity
I'm going to arrive in Naples
fully charged.

XX
We could have flown to Naples.
We could have walked to Rome.
All the roads lead there.
So many possibilities.

XXI
Addie's efforts to learn Italian
are not going as she would like,
I infer from what she is doing
with her hands and face.

XXII
There's the old aqueduct
or elevated train track again.
I'm not sure. No one ever told me.

XXIII
Addie wants fruit and doesn't know
if I'm being serious when I suggest
she can get one of Napoli's famous
Peach Pizzas!

XXIV
The Luperts have arrived in Naples!
Or at least we will in a few minutes.
I'm not going to have time to write this then.

In an Italian Taxi

Our taxi driver tells us
too many tourists in Naples
from the driver's seat of
his dented, cash-only taxi.

Too much good pizza
he tells us.
A problem I've been dreaming of having.

I Sea

If I am at all concerned Naples
wouldn't be as beautiful as Bologna
or Florence, all I need to do is look
out my hotel windows to the sea.
The beautiful sea.

In Another Italian Taxi

Our driver to *Piazza Dante*
gets into a loud conversation
with another taxi driver through
two sets of taxi windows.

Cars rule the city,

Addie notes in this city
with the largest historic center
and the beggar who touched her
with his golden microphone.

Free Walking Tour of Naples

I
The English free walking tour
was cancelled but they invite us
to join the tour for Spanish speaking
people which is also in English.

II
Addie, reading over my shoulders,
corrects me and says we were
invited to join a different English
speaking tour. Thank God my
shoulders are not so high
up in the air that Addie can't
see over them and tell me
what's what.

III
Carmen, our guide, is wearing black jeans
and wandering around Piazza Dante
in the sun. No hat or umbrella.
We're not sure she's human,
but she seems nice.

IV
She gives us
three thousand years of history
in two minutes.

V
Naples means *new city*.
The Greeks were original.

VI
It is hot in Dante's square
like in his inferno.

VII
Dante was the father of
the Italian language because
of *The Divine Comedy*.

VIII
Every city in Italy has to have
a *Piazza Dante*. I don't remember
if this is a real fact or if
I made it up.

IX
*Metro Toledo is the
most beautiful metro station in the world*
according to CNN
as reported by Carmen.

X
First stop on the tour:
a hole in a wall.

XI
Wallet pizza —
you fold it and put stuff in it.
But not money.
You can't eat that.

XII
Pita and pizza were sisters.

XIII
Calo = good pizza
Cato = bad pizza

XIV
They have good Neapolitan pizza in Brazil
which has more pizzerias than anywhere.

XV
We see the original Greek walls
which were destroyed to build
the new old city.

XVI
Mozart studied in Naples
where they had three hundred maestros
she tells us in front of the
Reggio Calabria Conservatorio di Musica.

XVII
The group breaks out into
O Sole Mio.

XVIII
Elvis sang *It's Now or Never*
to the tune of *O Sole Mio.*
Every city we go to
Elvis is with us.

XIX
The graffiti says *make love make love make love.*
They don't even bother with *not war.*
Italy is post *not war.*

XX
Gino Sorbillo Pizza is the best.

XXI
We touch Pulcinella's nose for
good luck and because
why not? It's free.

Carmen has touched his nose
so many times she may be
the luckiest person in Italy.

XXII
Nero declared that it wasn't an earthquake
but the Gods applauding him.

XXIII
There are many undergrounds to visit.
I may have bought tickets to the wrong one.

XXIV
I overhear someone on the tour say
I want pizza for dinner.

XXV
We see a real live Banksy.
Madonna With a Gun.

XXVI
I need to eat pizza fritta.
Fritta means fried.

XXVII
They put up a statue of San Gennaro
and faced it towards Mt. Vesuvius, which
promptly stopped erupting.

XXVIII
The treasure of San Gennaro
is owned by the Neapolitans
so Carmen can come take her share
if she falls on hard times.
Just kidding.

XXIX
You can only see the blood
of the saint once a year.
Solid or liquid form.

They're not sure it's a miracle
But it's, at least, tradition.

XXX
L'Antica Pizzeria da Michele
is the *Eat, Pray, Love* pizzeria
in a *forgettable neighborhood.*

XXXI
Spaccanapoli divides Naples in two.
On one side is the old city.
On the other is the modern.
Modern means two hundred years old.

XXXII
It's not a red chili. It's a horn
and it has its own laws.
It must be curvy.
You can't buy it for yourself.
But if you want one you can say
it's for a friend and the shop owner
will tell you it's his gift for you.
It may represent the
bloody finger of San Gennaro.

XXXIII
We pass by a store offering
Holes for the lobes.
So that's always an option.

XXXIV
Largo Corpo di Napoli —
The crocodile is missing from the statue.
The sphinx is still in good shape.

XXXV
Bar Naples houses the hair of
famous soccer player Maradona.
Maradona confirmed it was his hair.

XXXVI
The number one attraction on Tripadvisor
is the Sansevero Chapel museum where
we will find the *Veiled Christ.*

XXXVII
We end in
New Jesus Square.
But only the tour.
We begin all of Naples now.

XXXVIII
Whatever Carmen did over the last two hours
it leaves me weeping. Her passion
for this place she loves is now mine.

We're on Our Own Now

I walk in circles babbling in tongues
in New Jesus Square. Something has overcome me.
Also, the GPS isn't sure where I am yet.

At Gino Sorbillo

I couldn't be
more hungry
for this pizza.

Pulcinella's head
surveys the room.

Red wine to start so
by the time the pizza arrives
it will be religion.

We wonder if we should
lick the leftover pizza
so they can't serve it
to anyone else.

(Mainly I wondered that
out loud after finishing
the first pizza.)

The second pizza
is our server's favorite
summer pizza.

Must have been
confusing for him
when he asked

if we wanted a box
and I thought he was
pointing to his summer pie

and asking *the best*
when I pointed to the
empty plate where

the Margherita was
and said I preferred
that one.

The last four stanzas may
not be clear. Email me if
you need me to explain.

He offers Limoncello
and we are obligated to agree.
Now the Limoncello

is making me cry. Giuseppe says
this is the pizza of our life.
He touches his heart.

Back on the Street

I
A man is *spritz loud*.
Italians know how to use their voices
Addie says.

II
It's a fork and knife pizza kind of town
unless you're willing to
fold it like a pocket.

III
I am waiting for someone
to decline my offer of
Rickocello.

Driving in Naples

Gladiator-level madness.
Lights and pedestrians
not even suggestions.
Every thing for itself.

Goodnight Naples

One walking tour into Naples and
she has won me over. This historic center
which goes on forever, with unlimited
pizzas and Limoncello and things to
look up at, and down at, and all the
directions you can think of at. A city
of Italians built on a city of Romans
built on a city of Greeks. Three
completely different sets of Gods
still competing for my attention
in layers of stone. Just tonight I've
eaten so much pizza there is
enough of me for two Ricks
which is perfect because I'm
staying here and sending the
other one back to tend to all
the emails. Maybe, after enough
Sfogliatelle I'll have enough for
a third who can get another job
and finance this whole operation.
This whole operation is going to sleep
now to dream of putting lemons and
vodka and sugar into jars, and
making my fortune selling whatever
happens in four to six weeks.
Goodnight Naples. But not goodbye.
Never goodbye.

Naples Day 1

in which we are above and below ground

At Breakfast

I
Vesuvius surveys our breakfast at the Excelsior
ready to make its move. I'm hoping to
get through a double espresso before
anything happens. This view of the sea
is ready to take its turn at the Naples open mic
of grandiose things.

II
Addie doesn't like the cappuccino
she is brought. She claims it's
more like a latte and the milk
she says, seems *extra cow*.
I'm glad someone's getting any cow
out of this experience.

III
The unexpected bubbles in
our breakfast water has me
questioning everything I know
about the word *naturale*.

IV
Now I
am the
mug
licker.

V
They take my fork away
with my first plate.
You only get one chance
with a fork here.

VI
Still reading my empty
espresso mugs for signs
of what the day will bring.
This one mostly empty with
a ring around the middle.
Today will be like Saturn
if the planet left the rings
for parts unknown.

VII
Addie has already surveyed
the number of babies on this
breakfast terrace, so it's not
news to her when I point out
the visible feet on one of them.
She's more interested in the
tinier baby. Possibly cousins
with the feet baby, either way
destined to be best friends.
The tiny baby is *weeks old*
she says ... then acknowledges
we are all *weeks old*.

In Bourbon Tunnel

I
Built as an escape route for the king to the sea,
it was filled with garbage for twenty-five years.
It took seven years to empty.
They could have offered tourists
free historic garbage to get it done quicker.

II
It's a puppet, not a colleague of David
our guide, climbing up the wall.

III
The workers would climb up the private wells
of rich people and *make his own paycheck*
by stealing items there. Sometimes they might
drop something which the home owners would find
creating the legend of the little monk, Munaciello,
a ghost who would sometimes give and sometimes
take something.

IV
They weren't paid well.
Haha *well*.

V
The ice shavings cart is made of
many pieces of other things.

VI
The impound lot is filled with
vehicles which were too fast
for police vehicles to catch.

VII
Everything covered in
decades of rust.

VIII
Makeshift Harley Davidsons galore.

IX
The king told the people the tunnels would be
an underground shopping center. He lied.

X
Mechanical blinkers became illegal.
A driver would steal the newer lights
from newer cars and place them on his car,
but never connect them.

XI
The first imported car, a Chevy,
is down here. It had a radio!

XII
A siren goes off and I turn around
and put my hands against the wall
out of an abundance of caution.

XIII
Luxurious toilets underground
with seats and hinges for doors!

XIV
Getting a lot of ideas about the underground
tunnels I could build under our house in Newhall.

XV
He keeps telling us to watch out for the ceiling.
Does he have any idea who we are?

XVI
Another part of the tunnels
under poor people's homes —
just squatty toilets.

XVII
*We are not a museum of the ancient
but rather a museum of yesterday.*

XVIII
Walter Waschke spoke Neapolitan.
His father was a Polish soldier from World War I.
His name is carved on the wall.
They found his name in the phone book.
They called him and eighty-seven-year-old Walter
answered the phone.
He was five when he carved his name.

XIX
We could save them some time by writing
our names and phone numbers on the walls.
David doesn't recommend it.

XX
The tour is over and
we are nowhere near the exit.
David says he will lead us to
the promised exit.

XXI
Final thought —
there's a disturbing lack of bourbon
in the Bourbonica Tunnels.

A sign outside the Bourbon Tunnels

says *Quick No Problem Parking*.
It's a good service but more expensive
than the nearby *This Will Take an Hour
And We Will Pee on Your Car Parking*.

P.S. Nearby is "World's Coolest Car Parks."
I'm not sure I need an *experience* out of
parking my car.

In Another Italian Taxi

I
This taxi had no seatbelts and
the manual window rollers do nothing.
This man pulled this ancient taxi
right out of the tunnels before
picking us up.

II
He beeps his horn for no reason.
Or maybe he's signaling *solidarity*
to the cabby in front of us.

III
We drive by the famous hole
from yesterday.

Museo Archeologico Nazionale de Napoli

I
Apollo's got big toes.

II
Lots of friendly panthers and proof
that dogs have been man's best friend
for thousands of years.

III
Dionysus has grapes for hair
which would be better than what
I've got going on right now.

IV
Ganymede's best friend is an eagle.
I think sometimes they kiss.

V
Meleager with the head of a boat —
naked and proud of what he's done here.

VI
Picasso visited this museum and Pompeii
and they imply it may have influenced his work.

VII
Seated Woman
Picasso, 1929

She's got big feet and hands like the statues.
Must have been here in July, Addie says.

VIII
Hercules was found without legs.
Now the legs are on display.
Found them! I offer, helpfully.

IX
Addie stands in the hole
between the legs of the
So called Tiberius.

X
Many of these statues are called the "so called..."
It's very sarcastic here.

XI
Warrior with Child
2nd-3rd centuries

Never run with scissors.
Running with children, okay.

XII
The "Farnese Bull"
Apollonius of Tralles and Tauriskos of Tralles

I'd hate to have to pose
for a sculpture of this size.

XIII
If it's not *so called*
it's in quotes.

XIV
Minotaur With a Goblet in His Hand and a Young Woman
Picasso, May 1933

The bull and the lady chilling with a glass of wine
on a break from posing for the sculpture.

XV
I'd like to Photoshop my head
onto all the ancient headless statues
with my classic Caesar hairdo.

XVI
Casts of the Statues of the Goddess Hathor Protecting the High Dignitary Psammetichus, the Goddess ISIS and the God Osiris

Sir, would you like a hat
or an entire bull for your head?
Bull, please, Addie says.
Just be careful in the china shops.

XVII
If they weren't behind glass we could
make our fortune selling shabtis!

XVIII
She was only twenty-five years old
this mummy girl from 959-924 BC.
Never knew she'd be famous in Naples.

XIX
We see the jars of Payeftjauemawyaset. (664-525 BCE)
His organs are in there!

XX
Mummified crocodile (664-333 BCE)
with its mummified crocodile babies —
no descendants to carry on
its crocodile legacy.

XXI
These Egyptian miniatures are so well preserved,
unlike our objects today which disintegrate
upon first use.

XXII
An Egyptian chess set —
except all the pieces are the same
and instead of playing chess you
put them in your tomb.

XXIII
I have the simplest tastes.
I am always satisfied with the best.
~ Oscar Wilde from the *Mann Cafe* menu.

XXIV
"An Empire of Beauty"
First half of first century BCE

This is the mosaic I want them
to wrap up so I can take it with me.

XXV
Marine Life Mosaic
Early 1st Century BCE

The octopus gets all the attention.

XXVI
Theatrical mask
Early 1st Century BCE

Addie has found an Oompa Loompa!

XXVII
The tiles, so tiny in these
two thousand-year-old mosaics.
They look like paintings.

XXVIII
Everyday objects from Pompeii —
tools, statues, containers, bowls, pitchers,
bronzeware, jars, baskets, soup spoons,
ladles, egg cups, blown glass. Everything,
for everyday people's everyday needs,
frozen in lava in a historical instant.

XXIX
I keep losing Addie in the archaeology museum.
Hopefully they'll preserve her for the enjoyment
of future generations.

XXX
These paintings
look like paintings because
they are paintings.

Sansevero Chapel Museum

I
We wait outside to see our boy JC one more time.
This is the last of the churches on this trip. Carmen
told us, yesterday, he looks *simultaneously veiled
and with nothing on*. It's ironic they make you
cover yourself considering the display.
She promised us *magic*.

II
The *Veil of Christ* sculpture is described as
The cross contamination of life and death.

III
They also use the phrase
the anatomical machines.

Spritzing

I
I'm in my happy place which is anywhere
I am drinking a spritz. In this case it's Meloncello
which isn't on anyone's menu but should be.
I don't think I have room left in my bar at home
to add what will need to be added after this
spritz of a vacation.

II
Addie wants me to try all the
different shapes of crackers
in the bowl to determine if
they are all the same. I am
not going to do that.

III
We are heavily spritzing in Naples.
There is only one table in *Casa Capasso*

so it is easy to book up the place.
I don't know how they make their money

I just know he *just wants to be fair*
is what he says when he tells us how much

these things cost. It is not prime
spritz hour and as best we can tell

there is no line waiting for this single table.
So we linger and linger and eat these nuts.

It may be a two pizza evening because
there are only so many nights in Naples

and we have to get it all in our mouths
before we fly away.

At Night With Pizza

Waiting for a table
at the place where
Margherita pizza

was invented.
A Meloncello Spritz
is in my veins and

we will dine-in unlike
the citizens in the takeout
line which goes up the street

to where the city is divided in half.
This could take a while so
I may need wine to continue the magic

and fall in love with whoever
brings it to us. A platonic love
like one has for food —

food that invokes memory
when it touches our tongues.
I may use the words *tongue*

and *mouth* in my travel poems
too much, but one thing's for sure:
I'm not going to stop.

At L'Antica Pizzeria da Michele

I
They say this is where Margherita pizza was invented.
We're going to ask them to prove it and it will involve
carbon dating and DNA samples.

II
A nine-year-old with pizza tee shirt —
he wore the right shirt for this occasion.

III
I have to jiggle a lot in the men's bathroom
to fool the sensors and make sure the light
doesn't go out.

IV
This pizza is cheap.
5.5 euros per pie.
Any pie.

This is good for the people.

Taxi Again

Another cab ride —
another near-death experience
for everyone involved.

Goodnight Naples

This space is for the poem
I may have written at
the end of this day

which wasn't in the document
when I came back to it
months later.

If there was a poem.
I may have gone directly to sleep.
But that is unlikely.

So this space is for that poem
which I probably wrote, but
is now missing.

In case you see it
tuck it in here
where it belongs.

Naples Day 2

in which things happen you can read about on the following pages

Breakfast Next to the Sea

Breakfast affords a view of the bay,
the castle, the port, the volcano.

We move tables because the
smoking man is within his rights.

The instrumental notes and vocal tones
that make up, *you can ring my bell*,

create the soundtrack. That creation
comes from my favorite decade to

match music to movement.
I'm pacing myself at the buffet as

the timing of the deep fried pizza is
undetermined and will affect everything.

I go for water and Addie tells me to
shoot for *naturale* as yesterday

the surprise bubbles were not the end goal.
Even at the new table the smoking man

is winning. I'm going to finish this
double espresso, take my vitamins

accompanied by the still water
(I got it right!) and head to the opera

in the center of town to see whose
bell I can ring.

Addie Takes Over the Narrative

I forgot the green belt I bought in Hawaii
which is perfect and needed for these shorts
and now Addie is preparing her narration
*Rick Lupert walks out into the streets of
Naples without pants.* This was inevitable.
This was always going to happen.

Waiting for the Opera

I
This should actually be called
Waiting for the tour of the opera house.
There will be no opera today.

II
That guy in the flip-flops
is from Orange County.
How do I know?
He told me in the bathroom.

At the Opera

I
This should actually be called
At the Teatro di San Carlo, est. 1737.
There will be no opera today.

II
This is the oldest,
continuously operating opera
in the world.

III
The guide forgets to speak in English
and only the Italians follow him at first.

IV
An Italian *temple of opera.*

V
The Teatro San Bartolomeo was destroyed
by the order of the Bourbon King and its timber
was used to build this theater in a *more suitable location.*

VI
It took eight months to build and in November of 1937
the first opera was performed, written by Pietro Mascagni.

VII
One of the many restorations over the years
included an increase in the theater's incline to
improve visibility, much to the joy of
short opera fans who couldn't afford boxes.

VIII
Static on the microphone
makes her go rogue.

IX
A single candle
almost destroyed the theater
with the fire it made.

X
Many architects and artists
participated in the restorations
over the centuries.

XI
People who sit in the top are known as *pigeons*
as they were the most likely to make noise
like pigeons during the operas.

XII
A mermaid tries to stop time on the
non-functional clock in the proscenium arch
so the shows last longer.

XIII
More mermaids hold up the royal box.

XIV
Every seat has an air-conditioning hole under it.
The key words here are *air conditioning*
and *hole*.

XV
The number of candles in a box
indicated how prestigious you were.

XVI
The mirrors in each box, each at a specific angle,
allowed you to see the king which was important
as it was forbidden to begin applause until he did.

XVII
The royal box, today, seems reserved
for the sound person.

XVIII
It is rare that anything but opera
happens here, but it happens sometimes.
Last month Bono performed with a poet.
I missed my chance by one month.

XIX
King Charles was religious but superstitious.
There is no box 17 which is bad luck.
This only applies to the floor with the royal box.
Every other floor has to fend for itself.

XX
We are told to wait in the historic foyer.
This is where we will have our historic spritzes tonight
I tell Addie in my fancy voice.

XXI
At the end of the tour I begin the applause,
which lets everyone else know it is okay
to follow suit.

Assuming Responsibility

I ask a stray dog at the Dante metro station who appears to have just gotten off the train if I can see his ticket.

Raining Voice

In the alleyways of the *Centro Storica*
away from, but close to, where tourists walk,
from a balcony above, an Italian voice
falls on our heads out of a woman who
has been speaking the language since
Dante invented it. This is the
living *Divine Comedy*.

The Many Pregos

Prego, no marinara.
Prego, no Lego.
Prego, no leggo my Eggo.
Ego Nwodim.
Manchego!

Napoli Sotterranea

I
We walk down forty meters.
I'm not interested in walking back up
so I hope they have turndown service.

II
We are forty meters below
solidified lava, *tufa*.

III
The underground city looked like
layers of Swiss cheese — many holes.

IV
We are standing on top of rubbish.

V
Cholera was caused when humans
built a sewer system a level above
the aqueduct on the porous rock.

VI
More World War II toilets and showers.

VII
Luis has identified us as *short*
and is bringing us to the front.
A private tour in a giant's tour.

VIII
Two bombs intertwined and
the space wasn't wide enough
for them to reach the ground.

They never detonated.
Here they are. Don't worry
They've been deactivated.

IX
Luis tells the group we are his cousins
explaining why we are moved to the front.
He asks why we never visit and asks if
I brought him a present.

X
Originally only small people
could enter and leave.
These are our people.

XI
A hydroponic —
plants only watered when they're planted
then they absorb the humidity and thrive.
They turn the lights on at eight
and off at eight.

XII
Another group walks by us.
Luis tells us that they've been
looking for the exit for two weeks.

XIII
Now the man with the large backpack
has bumped into all the Luperts in Italy.

XIV
I hear water.

XV
Tunnels were narrow and curvy
so the water would travel faster.

XVI
Underwater well.
Clear water.
I ask him if there's

a changing room.
I brought my swimsuit.
Umbrella on water floor

I see the diving board.
Waiting for the last person
so Luis knows to speak.

XVII
Someone says
I'm too tall for this.
He is shorter than me.
He isn't old enough to
know his real height.

XVIII
He tells us *right, right, left*
before heading off into
another passage not meant
for Pavarotti. Also
turn your cell phone lights on.

XIX
I go into a long narration
about how they drop the pizza
down the wells and you point
your open-mouthed head up.
You have to ask to have a mozzarella
ball dropped separately, and if you
catch the whole thing in your mouth
you get a prize. They may still
put a ball on your pizza if you're lucky
so you'll get two balls.

XX
I can feel my pants falling down
these ancient wells.

XXI
Addie introduces the phrase
hole partner into the situation.

XXII
Don't write poetry
on ancient stairways.

XXIII
We enter street level
which isn't ancient and
where we walked for free
earlier.

XXIV
I get some ancient water
on my relatively new toe.

XXV
We enter a secret hole!

XXVI
Roman brickwork
from the first century
is pointed out
in Latin.

XXVII
What we see now —
the beauty of function.

XXVIII
We emerge from the ground
like a colony of ants
to the surprise of pedestrians.

XXIX
All these buildings
built on many
previous civilizations.

XXX
Every nondescript street doorway
could be a passageway to an
ancient Roman something or other.

XXXI
Every time they dig in Naples
they have to open a new museum.

XXXII
Nero performed here —
the lyre and song.
Then the earth shook.
He said it was the gods applauding.
But it was Vesuvius getting ready
to take Pompeii.

XXXIII
Nativity scenes all include
a hole to the city underneath
plus columns indicating the
triumph of Christianity
over paganism.

XXXIV
One last bit of wisdom from Luis:
Eat pizza in the *Centro Storica*
on the two main streets.
The farther away you go the
less good and more expensive it is.
He says the people aren't as smart either.
We ask him where he lives and
he says *farther away.*

Antica Pizzeria De Figliole

This can't possibly be good for me.
But it is good for me
if you know what I mean.

Guy Driving a Vespa Down Spaccanapoli

One hand and two eyes
on his cellphone.
Doing his best to
win a Darwin Award.

Kebap

You can get a kebab in Naples but if you want a kebap you have to go to Reggio Emilia.

Spritz O'Clock

I
Pigeons walk the marbled floor in front of
Bar Brasiliano in Galleria Umberto
while we wait for two different spritzes
to come to our table. One *Apérol* and
one *Limoncello,* if you must know.

II
Addie manages to make *spritz*
sound Yiddish which I think
was how Yiddish was invented
in the first place.

III
*Don't fly away from me when
I'm talking to you* I tell the pigeon
after I started to ask it if it knew
the pigeons from St. Mark's Square
in Venice.

IV
You can walk the streets with
spritzes to go. Italy is the open
carry Vegas of the Mediterranean.

At the Pizza-Making Class in Pizzeria Trattoria San Carlo

One man is excited to put on
his plastic apron.

Meanwhile, we haven't
been given them.

The dough is seventy percent water
like the human body.

Manuela tells me she will fix
my wet dough.

I end up finishing first and
am sent to wash my hands.

But, not before I drop the dough
on the floor.

I fall for her trap when she asks
how we flatten the dough.

She made rolling pin motions
so I said *rolling pin.*

But the correct answer is *by hand.*
Now go to the table, Manuela says,

There is bruschetta waiting for you.
Manuela brings our doughs upstairs.

Tells us to follow when ready.
Addie is confident they are

throwing our doughs away.
I think they're proofing them for

tomorrow's guests.
The temperature upstairs

is like one of Dante's Hells, so
she only takes a few people

up at a time. She had to help me
put on the apron as unfolding it

was a task beyond my abilities.
Addie is looking forward to

me making dough when we
get home. She's willing to, maybe,

make the sauce. I took off my
wedding ring for this. But only for this.

A full red wine later and I am fully
ready to walk up the stairs

for whatever happens up there.
They're walking down the stairs

with fully cooked pizzas. Now I
know what happens up there.

What happens upstairs stays upstairs.
Until we bring it down. Not the exact

pizza we made, but one from our
group of four. A Spanish man is eating

my pizza with less cheese and
carefully placed basil. Manuela says

Addie could be French, like
Breakfast at Tiffany's. She'll take it.

We take half of two pizzas to go
though God knows when we'll eat them.

Pizza makers are being replaced by
pizza diners — just people off the street

who have no idea what Manuela
told us today.

Goodnight Napoli

It's ambitious to wander around Naples.
Things aren't as close as they seem and
other things are surprisingly close.

Lemons are everywhere.
Red horns are everywhere.
Pulcinella is everywhere.

Opportunities to appear in
the background of other people's photos
are everywhere.

We started this adventure
a thousand years ago
or so our legs tell us.

I hope, when all is eaten and done,
when our butts are resting in flight
there isn't a rock concert on the plane.

We're going to need all that time
for shut-eye. That's still a few days away
and we have a whole other Paris to visit.

In the meantime, the Naples Bay will
lull us to sleep with its concert of waves
and tomorrow, we'll see what a volcano did.

Naples Day 3

in which we go to Pompeii and something about lemons

Buongiorno Napoli

This morning my empty double espresso mug
told me: *Broken hat* and *you can't ignore
Vesuvius anymore.* I had to read it quickly as

just seconds ago they took the mug away
with a smile that may have indicated they
knew what they were doing. I look up at

the volcano which I can see from the
breakfast terrace which is already a
significant thing to type out loud. Addie

is working her way through regional pastries
and today there are berries which has
never happened to us in this situation

in this city and we believe with all our
tired legs and hearts, this is Vesuvius' way
of offering empathy for my broken hat.

In My Eyes, Over the Sea

I see Motor Boat City
developing under seagulls
and just over this moist
regional pastry.

To Amalfi

I
Walking away from our hotel
Addie spots a man in a suit
and suggests we walk toward him.
We do and a few feet away he
spots us and asks *Lupert?*
Everyone should have the
experience of having strangers
in a strange land greet you
by name. His name is Paulo
and immediately he is
no longer a stranger.

II
Pompeii is *oh my God*
Naples is *mamma mia*
Paulo tells us.

III
He gives us free water bottles.
This tour is already paying
for itself.

IV
Always count on a
man in a suit to take you
where you want to go.

V
Concetta gets on the bus.
She says to call her *Titti*.

VI
Paulo tells us an amusement park
is a *town of the babies*.

VII
Titti gives us a bracelet with her
name and phone number on it
but clarifies we can only use it today.

VIII
Paulo jokes it's his first day on the job
but that means his record is spotless.

IX
Four English hooligans get on the bus.
I plan on breaking the ice by talking
about *Doctor Who* with them.

X
A family with a baby gets on the bus.
I hope that baby has a baby hat.

XI
Vesuvius is the *King of Naples*.

XII
Titti keeps asking if we can hear her.
We keep saying *no*. Italian tour guides
do not know how to use microphones.

XIII
79 A.D. is when
it all went down.

XIV
This is an air-conditioned bus.
The term *air-conditioned* is
used loosely.

XV
Vesuvius last erupted in 1942.
These were its efforts to rid Italy of Nazis.
Like the *big one* we're waiting for in California,
Vesuvius is overdue. Its next eruption will
be an explosion and not a simple lava flow
Titti tells us. *But don't worry it's
not scheduled for today.*

XVI
In front of us are the Milky Mountains.
Behind them is Amalfi.

XVII
Surprise Limoncello factory stop!
Beautiful views of Sorrento.
One could drop one's phone
into lower Sorrento from this place.
Titti rolls her r's like a professional.
We try everything they offer.
If you get the tourists drunk
at the beginning of the tour
it's easier to make them happy
the rest of the day.

XVIII
A very careful older woman
rides a Vespa in front of us
along the Amalfi Coast.

XIX
I am sweating on this
air-conditioned bus.

XX
Poseidon named *Positano*
after one of his girlfriends.

XXI
We stop to take pictures of
the colorful houses of Positano
and the sea that looks at them.

XXII
There is a stairway with
seventeen hundred steps here.
I don't know where it leads to
or where it comes from, but
seventeen hundred steps
just got added to my bucket list.

XXIII
Paulo honks his horn to indicate
his displeasure. Another car honks back
and now the cars are having a dialogue
in their own special language.

XXIV
Praiano is the *heart of Amalfi*.
In this heat it may soon be the
heart attack of Amalfi.

XXV
We enter Funnoa (the sound the sea makes
as it crashes into the rocks), also known as
the city that doesn't exist.

Addie wants to know how I feel being
in a town that doesn't exist.
*It's a good place a man can
disappear* I tell her.

XXVI
We pass by the Fjord of Funnoa.
I wonder if it exists.

XXVII
Paulo waves to a man standing
in front of a ceramics shop which
seems to confuse the man.

XXVIII
We pass by the Amalfi hotel
where Brad Pitt and Angelina Jolie
spent their honeymoon.

Seeing how it worked out for them
this is not the best endorsement
for this hotel.

XXIX
If I met Brad Pitt the first thing I would say is
I would like to talk with you about Fight Club.

XXX
Waiting for lemon pasta on Amalfi —
it is not twelve yet. *You can sit and
at twelve you will eat.*

The internet does not know I am here.
This is risky — the amount of time we have
and the amount of time it may take.

The server tells us not to worry
but I am a worrier when it comes to
needing to be places at times.

I want to be the best citizen of the clock
so when they write my final story
it will be exactly when it should be.

XXXI
Up the ancient staircases
the sign says and I am only
too happy to oblige.

XXXII
What was promised as an
enchanting regional dining experience
became stressful when the food took
until the end of time to get to us.

XXXIII
I would have liked to have gotten
a lemon sorbet served in an
actual lemon but Poseidon
was not on our side today.

XXXIV
Atrani is the smallest village in Italy.
I feel you, Atrani.

XXXV
Everything is precariously on a cliff
in this part of Italy. Thank you
cousin Rachel for giving me the word
precariously for this situation.

XXXVI
We are now in the highest peak of Amalfi.
And now we are in a tunnel
leaving Amalfi behind.

To Pompei

I
According to a climate expert on CNN
Italy has turned into a *giant pizza oven.*
That's an official meteorological term.

II
So just one pizza tonight
I tell Addie, both of us stuffed
with lemon pasta winding
down a mountain road
which gets me the look
I was hoping for and then a
*don't talk to me about pizza
right now. You must get me
lemon sorbetto as soon as possible.*

III
I bought a bucket hat with lemon drawings on it.
I plan on being both practical and ridiculous in Pompeii.

IV
What's in this truck will kill your fish is,
I assume, what one warning sign tells us.

V
We arrive at Pompeii Archaeological Site
which begins with markets and cold things.
I hope it ends with them as well.

VI
The water is not potable.
I hope it is put on my faceable.

VII
Ana, our guide, has what I assume
are Pompeiian frills on her sleeves.

VIII
Pompeii is famous for its last days.
Pompeii was a festival to worship Hercules.
We stand in the shade of umbrella palm trees.

IX
It started at nine in the morning
which is earlier than I'd want to start.

X
Ana is an archaeologist.

XI
The Romans didn't realize
Vesuvius was a volcano.

XII
We see examples of Times New Roman font.
They practically invented word processing here.

XIII
They found the nine a.m. bread, flat like pita…pizza.

XIV
Drinking wine was very important to the Romans.
But forbidden for women.

XV
I'm walking over chariot grooves.

XVI
All of this used to be underground.

XVII
The Egyptians were here too as evidenced
by their symbology in the frescoes.

XVIII
I take a photo of the Greek poet Menander.
He was famous for comedies. Ana starts to
tell us about a tragic poet but I'm less interested.

XIX
Addie finds the original Pac-Man mosaic floor.

XX
We see the skeletons of
people who came after to
steal silver from rich people's houses
who died while there because of noxious fumes.
Addie and I place stones anyway.

XXI
We pass by an unexcavated area.
Always more to do.

XXII
Don't write poetry while walking
on uneven Roman Streets.
Not even in the chariot tracks.

XXIII
Vesuvius hasn't changed as much as this city has.

XXIV
They used lead pipes
which led to shorter lives
but many of them died
even faster than that.

XXV
The Roman spa opens at noon.
I mean it did.

XXVI
Bodies dissolved instantly.
Human cavities found.
Casts made so you can see
their final fetal positions.

XXVII
We enter the red light district
Dicks on the wall indicate
where you are.

XXVIII
The *Lupanare* is what the brothel is called.
This is one of my family's proudest moments.

XXIX
Pompeii was bombed in 1942.
Hadn't they endured enough?

XXX
The brothel was at the intersection of three roads.
Tri Via. Trivia.

XXXI
The four hoodlums on the trip
really come alive in the whorehouse.
Though I think they're disappointed it's closed.

XXXII
Oh, and there was a tsunami in the same year
which destroyed the port.

XXXIII
In Naples, the Roman city is
under the buildings of the new old city.
In Pompeii the volcano preserved the old
and nothing was built on top.

We get to see ancient frescoes,
perfectly preserved mosaic floors,
ancient dicks in walls pointing the way,
and the shapes of those who had
no idea what came.

I Can Feel This

We are leaving Italy tomorrow.
All of this will crash to an end.
Shut up. We're going to Paris.

A much-needed siesta

(which may be called something
different here) in the hotel after

sweating out all our liquid in Pompeii.
Strategic choices are made from the

dwindling supply of clean clothing.
Who's going to smell us, anyway

except each other and we're in this for life
no matter the smells. It's *spritz o'clock* again

and then our last pizza in Italy
at the place where Margherita was invented —

The pizza type, not the lady.
Maybe she's from here too.

It would make sense that the pie
was named after someone.

At the Place Where Margherita Pizza Was Invented

Brandi — Our last pizza in Italy.
Not crowded, but better than the ones

we made ourselves last night.
They cut it in half for us!

We could almost pick it up.
No need for forks and knives.

As if they knew we were going home
soon and they wanted to ease us into it.

Addie wishes she was hungry enough
to get eggplant parmesan.

But that's not why we are here.
A pizza every night for four nights —

that's why we are here.
No need to eat again.

All the Pizza Restaurants Are a Stage

A little kid at the other table
who I've been performing for *all pizza*
just dropped his stuffed rabbit on the floor.

He dropped it again. He dropped it again.
He dropped it again. Now he's trying to
stick the bottle cap on his forehead like I did.

That four year old is my new best friend.
My body is still working through the
Limoncello spritz from the other place.

Last Limoncello

Rooftop.
There is Vesuvius.
There is Sorrento.

Music below. Live.
The bay.
The Naples Bay.

We are now
ninety-three percent pizza.
Seven percent Limoncello.

Whatever came before
is for them to discover
in the future.

Buona Notte Napoli

I fell asleep almost before writing this
and doing all the things I needed to do
before the day ended.

Can you imagine if tomorrow came and
these words had never been assembled
for you to read?

Good night to you ... and one last time
to Naples, and all of Italy. We fly to
another country tomorrow,

just to be indulgent
just for the *why not* of it.
Buona notte ...

A Day in Which We Travel From Italy to France

especially the Paris part of France

The Unbearable Passage of Time

All units of time are awkward
when you are aware of them
so, it is nothing special that we
have an awkward amount of time
before we need to leave for the airport.
Too little to do something.
Too much to not do something.
Even if we extend breakfast
beyond its natural boundaries
the seconds will not change
the way they turn into minutes
and we will be extra aware
of it happening. This is our burden
this morning as we transition
from Italy to France, all too slowly.

Shirtplomacy

I'm wearing a red shirt today
as France and Italy share that color
in their flags and my white shirts
are too infused with the sweat
of Italy to be good for anyone.

The Forever Breakfast

I
From the breakfast roof we
can see a boat surrounded by
smaller boats with tourists on them
preparing for their experience.
The orientation seems to go on
for a while and I wonder if
it's just a boat-top lecture
experience and they won't get
to small-boat paddle themselves
all the way to Sorrento.

II
Today my finished double espresso mug
looks like the bay of Naples. Even the
coffee, no, *especially* the coffee,
is pushing the momentous nostalgia
I feel at every possible transition.

III
Turns out there was one more sip
gathering in my espresso mug and
now I'm not sure where it looks like.

IV
Follow up on the boat's situation:
Addie suggests they might be fishing.
I think this whole scene would be
better if they added a lot of sea lions.

V
That big boat has been out there
since we arrived, I think, but then
am distracted by the photo of my cat screensaver
on my phone which I hold up towards the sea
in case anyone on the far away boat is observing
our breakfast and thinking *those two
have been there since we arrived.*

VI
Ring My Bell comes on again
and now we have come full circle
and they are resetting the entire
Napolese experience for the next
couple of Luperts to arrive.

VII
Addie points out the leaning tower of jam
and I use the opportunity to use my new
knowledge of archaeology to explain how
the original architects didn't know what
they were doing and these jams were
precariously like this for hundreds of years
before it became the major attraction it is today.

VIII
We spend an inordinate amount of time
at the breakfast buffet. The boats don't move.
The breakfast buffet becomes a restaurant
before our eyes. We can sit here as long
as we want but the food is *no longer possible.*
I communicate this by hand signals to the people
watching us from the far away big boat.
I have all the time in the world this morning,
to make their job as easy as possible.

IX
If you were to put this down
walk around for an hour and a half
pick this up again, only to realize
you had another hour, you'd get a sense
of this awkward amount of time.

Italian Denouement in the Excelsior Lobby

I
I'm dressed for walking around Naples
not riding on a plane. My pants are not
the right length. Socks either. This is
the product of an amount of time
we did not know what we would do with.

II
My whole plan for the last ten minutes
in the hotel lobby before our cab was
a single round of *Rock, Paper, Scissors*.
It did not take as long as I'd hoped.

III
Fabrizio thinks we are nice people.
We think he is a nice person.
More sadness leaving Naples.

Taxi Ride to the Airport

I
Oh, no! I left my *joie de vivre*
on top of the tower in Pisa!
We have to go back!

II
I would, a hundred percent,
die on a Vespa in Napoli.

III
I'm mixing accents
Italian and French and
maybe a little Hebrew
as I give Addie a tour
of the castle we are driving by.

*There are some bricks
and, if you look over there,
there are some other bricks.
Don't forget to tip your guide.*

Addie reacts in no way at all
to this tour.

IV
We are driving by a barbershop called
Hair on Top. Sounds like they
know what they're doing.

V
They haven't updated the roads here
since medieval times. Every part of me
is jiggling.

EasyJet Not Easy

They'll tell you the gate later.
Not easy.

One jiggle will make the auto-bag drop malfunction.
Not easy.

Their air-conditioning does not condition the air.
Not easy.

Stand in the hundred-degree direct sunlight.
Not easy.

No place to plug things in.
Not easy.

To Paris, as It Always Should Be

I
Now we are the people
on the plane to Paris
from Napoli.

II
From the plane window I can see our hotel
(and all of Naples) *arrivederci Fabrizio* —
you were the best.

III
People coughing on every flight.
On every bus.
The world is not healthy.

IV
Another possible title for this book
would be *The Italian Spritz*

or *It's Spritz O'Clock Somewhere*.

V
Paris, are you
under these clouds?

VI
I don't see Paris.
Does this guy know
where he's going?

In a Parisian Taxi

I can see the Eiffel Tower
from the window.

Looks like the pilot knew
what he was doing after all.

EasyJet:
Easy.

Paris seems to make sense

over the chaos of Naples.
I loved the chaos but it's nice
to not be taking my life into
my hands in a car or on the streets.
This calm sophistication is
exactly what we need.

Kimpton St. Honoré Paris

I am drinking Paris tap water
in my Paris hotel room.

The Eiffel Tower is outside
the window in reach of my eyes.

This room has secret passages.
I've already slinked through.

I've already angled my body to
pass by the slanted wall by the window.

We are near a rooftop of Paris.
Under one too. The light switches

couldn't be cuter.

Waiting for Refuge des Fondus to Open

Across the street, *La Vache et le Cuisinier* —
The Cow and the Kitchen.
I'm going to ask if I can meet the cow.
The kitchen is not necessary.

At Refuge des Fondus Again

I
I first came to this restaurant
twenty-eight years ago. Most of
the people in this line don't look
like they're twenty-eight years old yet.

II
Now you get a choice of who climbs
to take the interior seats. It's not
automatically the woman.

III
The toilet has been seriously upgraded.

IV
The kir isn't rimmed with sugar.
Addie says it was never rimmed.
I know for a fact it was rimmed.

V
I've also been coming to this restaurant
since before any of the staff were alive.
Rim the kir goddammit! I yell to them with
the seniority these decades have earned.

VI
Addie tends to the cheese
so it doesn't solidify as the
wine separates from it.
They should pay her.

VII
I've been here five times.
Most people here have never
been here once. Unless you
count today.

VIII
Addie waggles her finger
to indicate *no*. She has had
so many occasions to do this
based upon my behavior.
But mainly she's a fantastic
finger waggler.

IX
Tamina tells us the history.
This place started in 1966
by Jeannine, an Egyptian woman.
You always stepped over the tables
and the wine was always full.
The current owners bought it
in 2020.

X
I've lost my napkin three times
so far. But it always returns home.

XI
Since we are on the end I can
pull out the table so Addie can
use the facilities, thus changing
the historical nature of this
restaurant's setup.

XII
Rum and hibiscus digestif.
That's new!

XIII
Addie starts singing the
rubber ducky song after
I quack for some reason.

XIV
When I'm seventy-four
and bald
I'll be at the front
of the line to eat
at Refuge des Fondus.

XV
I tell one of the servers
I was here in 1995.
I was not alive, he says.

XVI
I love Paris.

We Put Things in Our Mouths

page 85, circa 2010

I want to wander around
Place du Tertre and ask
if anyone has seen a man
with a giant toothbrush.

Goodnight Paris

It is a dream to be in Paris.
This perfect, imperfect city.
Other cities are beautiful
but Paris is *beautiful*.
Since I first learned you
could cross the ocean
I dreamed of Paris.
I dream of Paris while
my feet are touching Paris.
This is a waking dream.
These streets. This French.
I dream of tomorrow's baguette.
I dream of the *Water Lilies*
the Latin Quarter
the ancient, brand new Notre Dame.
I dreamed of Paris years ago
and then fewer years ago
and today. My heart. This coffee.
These lights, spinning on top of
the tower to let everyone know.
Wake up, or never wake up.
It's fine. You are here, or you
should come here. Paris has
always been the dream.

A Day in Paris

as an example to all other days

Not Ordinary

A tip in a guide says *another ordinary picture of the Eiffel Tower — try something new.*

I wake up in Paris with that ordinary beauty staring at me through this French window.

The way she pierces the sky and stands assuming above everything else created

in this land of cheese and beautiful streets. We will wander all of them today, our only

day here, like it's the infusion we've needed for years to tide us over until the next time

we are lucky enough to *why not* our way across the sea to this place. Monet,

we are coming for you today. Seine, we will touch lips on your bridges.

Notre Dame, our much needed checkup after your disaster is on the schedule.

All of it in our eyes in one day. There are no *ordinary* pictures of the Eiffel Tower.

Quote Me

If you think there are ordinary pictures of the Eiffel Tower, you may have the wrong eyes.

Coffee and Pain au Chocolat at Ladurée

Soft chocolate and towers of macarons —
Addie states *no coconut* explaining
the difference between the *maca* pastries.
roons vs *rons*. The other one, this one
has almond paste. I point out these
are *little dessert sandwiches*. Before
we can get too much further, she
high pitch shrieks *stop what you're doing
right now* to make sure I see the mini
baguette that arrived at the next table.
Anything *mini* excites Addie. The woman
at the mini baguette table may be a blogger.
Her companion films her saying something
in a language we can't identify. The woman
running the show makes sure workers don't
stop directly in front of the entranceway.
She's young but has everything under control.
We're going to be okay today.

Macarons

Addie asks me to lean in and say *macarons*. *Closer* she says after the first time and almost doesn't reward me with a kiss. She got what she needed.

No Guillotining, Please

At the Place de la Concorde I tell Addie
this obélisque is where the guillotine was.
They used to chop people's heads off right there.
I'm glad they changed it into that instead, Addie says.

At the Musée de l'Orangerie

I
Les Adolescents
Picasso, 1906

Nu Sur Fond Rouge
Picasso, 1906

Equal opportunity nudes
was Picasso's motto.

II
Grand Baigneuse
Picasso, 1921

Painted as if she was a sculpture —
don't be afraid of her big feet.

III
Grand Nature Norte
Picasso, 1917-1918

This still life seems to come to life.
Could be the coffee and small amount
of sleep making this happen.

IV
They do not translate the painting titles here.
You must experience them as intended.

V
Lo Noce
Henri Rousseau, 1905

The best mustaches in town came to this wedding.

VI
A man tells his child
desperately in need of something
to *look at all the colors.*
He says it four times.

VII
I want everything I own
to be framed as ornately
as the paintings here.

VIII
Renoir painted his son Claude
many times. In one, he's a clown.
In another, a girl.

IX
Pommes et Poires
Renoir, 1899-1895

Pêches
Renoir, 1881-1882

Apples and pears share a painting.
Peaches get their own.

X
Portrait de Madame Cézanne
Cezanne, 1890

Madame Cézanne au jardin
Cezanne, 1879-1880

Mrs. Cezanne lost some weight
between these two paintings.

XI
There are narrations for children
by many of the paintings which
pleases all the Addies in the room.

XII
This is my
favorite museum
in the world.

XIII
Danseuses espagnoles
Marie Laurencin
Paris, 1883-1956

Three dancers have a party
with a horse and a dog.
You're invited.

XIV
Portrait de femme à la colombe
Marie Laurencin, 1932

We may never know what is
being communicated between
the woman from Colombia
and the dove.

XV
Derain is the best represented artist
in the museum. His more traditional style
was not a "return to order," but a
reconnection to the past.

XVI
La Nièce du peintre assise
André Derain, 1931

Do I have to visit uncle André again?
He's just going to want to paint me.

XVII
Les Pêcheurs à la ligne
Henri Rousseau, 1908-1909

No one mentions the airplane.

XVIII
La Carriole du Père Junier
Rousseau, 1908

Three dogs in this picture.
The smallest one, the horses
consider eating. Only one
gets to ride in the carriage with
the fantastic mustache people.

XIX
Most of the animals Soutine painted were dead —
the rabbit, the pheasant, the turkey.
Still life.

XX
Garçon d'honneur
Soutine, 1924-25

Man of honor —
taking advantage of his position
with his wide open legs.

XXI
We look at all the other paintings
before the Water Lilies. It would
be unfair to look at them after the
indelible Monets go in our eyes.

XXII
The Nymphéas are
right where we left them
ten years ago.

Do you know the sound for *quack* in French?

I'm being serious.

A Star Trek Reference To Please That Demographic

Bjorg cookies in the supermarché —
resistance is delicious.

Lioness in Berlin

At lunch we hear the news of a
suspected lioness on the loose in Berlin.
As far as I'm concerned, it's innocent
until proven *lioness*.

At Le Pave

The plate of the day
is dependent on
the chef's mood.
I wonder what he serves
when he's angry.
(Or she.)

Kabob Bop

They have a *Maison du Kebab* in the Latin Quarter. If you want a *Maison du Kabop* you have to go to Reggio Emilia.

We stop for kir

and what must be a Sprite at *La Gentilhommiere*
in Saint André des Arts. The kir is good and our legs
appreciate the sit after the device tells us we've
walked over six miles today. This is not the end.
We're going to see every inch of Paris in this
one day we have. I would live here.
At this moment, I live here.

Notre-Dame de Paris

Notre-Dame is covered almost everywhere
with scaffolding. It's encouraging since the
last views I saw were of it burning on the TV.
We're past the destruction and it's going up again.
Maybe a couple more years and it will
again be one of the hearts of the city.

Current Crepe Situation

We're relieved that *Crêperie des Arts* is still here
and open after something on the web told us
it was permanently closed. A cat used to live
in there and you could pet it while you ate crepes.
I don't know the current cat situation
but the current crepe situation is strong.

I Prefer Bees

A bee buzzes our drinks and we wildly
flail it away as a smoking woman walks by.
She thinks we are waving her away and we
assure her it's just the bee. But then she
sits down next to us, smoking, and she
has, indeed, waved us away.

At the D'Orsay

I
We didn't think we'd be doing two museums today
but as they say *why not?*

II
Where they take your tickets I thought
she was gesturing for me to scan my own ticket
so I did and then she indicated that was weird
and scanned Addie's ticket. I haven't learned
French gestures yet. I wonder if I can get a discount
for scanning my own ticket. There's no one to ask
this side of the entry so I guess I'll just go look at more art.

III
We stop in the cat room
to see all the cat sketches.
Every single one of them.

IV
We do our best to recreate a photo from 2004
in front of a particular Monet Water Lilies
with Addie facing it, her bundles not as tight
as they used to be, but still as cute as
the cats in the room we saw earlier.

V
Starry Night has a *Birth of Venus* level
emotional pull on me.

VI
Addie's *Tide To Go* stick rolls out of her purse
in the Van Gogh room. Finally we can clean
the colors off all these paintings!

VII
I want to meet the Cabbage Fairy.

VIII
After watching a lady pull babies out of
a cabbage patch in the film *The Cabbage Fairy*
I finally know how babies are made.

IX
I want to apologize to the woman
whose job I usurped when I
scanned my own entry ticket.

Secret Knowledge

The train we're on goes by a place called *The Starving Club.* The first rule of Starving Club is you don't order pizza at Starving Club.

Crepes Over Champs

The extra museum visit threw off the timing
and we had to give up the Arc de Triomphe
and Champs-Élysées in favor of dinner.
That's okay. Those places continue to exist
without us. We returned to Crêperie des Arts
where we've been before and where sweet
and savory crepes make us feel like we've
made the right decision. Thank God for Paris
and its trains and its food and its river.
Thank God for all of Paris.

Parapluie

It just started raining in the Latin Quarter
and probably all of Paris. This is what happens
when you end a vacation without permission
from the European countries you are visiting.

Paris Is the Dream

If you think you should try to fit all of Paris
into a single day you are right and wrong.

You are right because it is Paris and if you
only have one day you should spend every

minute of it awake and ingesting this city.
Wrong because you should have planned

on being in Paris much longer than this.
Paris is best done over the course of a lifetime.

You'll need three years just for the river.
You'll need to sell everything and replace

it all with Parisian things. Paris is what
you will eat and breathe going forward.

Paris is the source of all beautiful poems.
The guidebooks say a week will do it.

My guidebook says this is your life now.
That's the dream, anyway.

I Go Home Now

I don't want to

At Breakfast

I
I respond to the host's *bonjour*
in Hebrew. It's that early and I'm that tired.
The espressos come just in time to help.
Addie likes the mugs. We have a long history
of mugs in this city.

II
This morning's empty espresso mug
is hard to read because of the dark
ceramic. We're leaving Paris today.
The future is uncertain.

This Is a Mistake

The rain during the short walk to the train says to us *why not go back inside. You don't want to get wet. Leaving Paris is always a mistake.*

Merci de Nous Céder Ces Places

Thank you for giving us these places

The man with no leg
The man with a cane
The man with a baby
The man with a baby inside her
The hunchback

At the Airport

I
The one that didn't
feel like I was cattle
unlike all the other airports
a young man plays the piano.
Bohemian Rhapsody
then *Hey Jude.* Hey Jude —
we're flying over the ocean
to see you. We'll make it
better together.

II
Nothing is free
at Duty Free.

III
In the waiting area we move seats
to be at an electric outlet that works.
But I think we insulted the man who
was sitting next to us at the old seat
who has no idea why we left him.

IV
At the El Al gate nearby they offer
PlayStation use for premium class passengers.
I can only imagine the security check
required after playing *Call of Duty.*

V
The gate announcements are only in French
here in Paris on Air Tahiti Nui to Los Angeles.
I hope my interpretation of what they're
asking us to do does not create an
international incident.

VI
That's right, *Air Tahiti Nui*.
If we refuse to get off the plane
we get a free trip to Tahiti.

VII
Nobody wears masks anymore.
We are all breathing each other's air.

VIII
Paper boarding passes.
This is how cavemen used to
fly to Tahiti.

On the Plane

I
The magazine is called
Paris Vous Aime
Paris You Love.
It knows.

II
One last view of the Eiffel Tower
from the Moana cabin until the plane
turns north to eventually pierce the
top of Greenland. We are three minutes
closer to Los Angeles. A bientôt, Paris.
Until we meet again.

Freeway

I am on the ground in Los Angeles
and the 405 is making sure that I
take it all in. It is Friday afternoon.
Everybody is in a rush and no one can rush.
This is the final insult of having to leave Europe.

Digestif

Here in Los Angeles I am wearing
a t-shirt I put on yesterday in Paris.
Socks too.

I was awake for twenty-four hours
and although my head's eyes first
opened in France

they didn't close until my head
hit the pillow in Southern California.
They want to close again now

because the world is large and
divided by a daylight and a night
that circle the world

and appear differently to everyone
depending on where they are.
I'm barely aware of

what *o'clock* it is and am trying
to stay awake as if I've always
been here.

Tomorrow we pick up the child
from the hills. We're going to
measure the sound

when he returns so we can
document the difference between
then and now.

Enjoy this last page. I'll write more
in the future from other places.
No one wants a thing to end.

This thing has ended.
I've already shaved Italy
and Paris into the sink.

I'll shower the rest away
soon enough. This shirt will
be the last of it.

For now.

Rick Lupert will return ...
possibly with a live moose.

About The Author

The author enjoying a *spritz* with his beloved in Modena, Italy

Three-time Pushcart Prize and Best of the Net nominee Rick Lupert has been involved with poetry in Los Angeles since 1990. He was awarded the Beyond Baroque Distinguished Service Award in 2014 for service to the Los Angeles poetry community. He served for two years as a co-director of the nonprofit literary organization Valley Contemporary Poets. His poetry has appeared in numerous magazines and literary journals, including *The Los Angeles Times, Rattle, Chiron Review, Red Fez, Zuzu's Petals, Stirring, The Bicycle Review, Caffeine Magazine, Blue Satellite* and others. He edited the anthologies *A Poet's Siddur: Shabbat Evening - Liturgy Through the Eyes of Poets, Ekphrastia Gone Wild - Poems Inspired by Art, A Poet's Haggadah: Passover Through the Eyes of Poets*, and *The Night Goes on All Night - Noir Inspired Poetry*. He is the author of twenty-seven other books: *The Low Country Shvitz, I Am Not Writing a Book of Poems in Hawaii, The Tokyo-Van Nuys Express, Hunka Hunka Howdee!, 17 Holy Syllables, God Wrestler: A Poem for Every Torah Portion* (Ain't Got No Press), *Beautiful Mistakes, Donut Famine, Romancing the Blarney Stone, Professor Clown on Parade, Making Love to the 50 Ft. Woman, The Gettysburg Undress* (Rothco Press), *Nothing in New England Is New, Death of a Mauve Bat, Sinzibuckwud!, We Put Things In Our Mouths, Paris: It's the Cheese, I Am My Own Orange County, Mowing Fargo, I'm a Jew, Are You?, Feeding Holy Cats, Stolen Mummies, I'd Like to Bake Your Goods, A Man With No Teeth Serves Us Breakfast* (Ain't Got No Press), *Lizard King of the Laundromat, Brendan Constantine Is My Kind of Town* (Inevitable Press) and *Up Liberty's Skirt* (Cassowary Press), and the spoken word album *Rick Lupert Live and Dead* (Ain't Got No Press). He hosted the long running Cobalt Café reading series in Canoga Park for almost twenty-one years, relaunched in 2020 as a virtual series, and has read his poetry all over the world.

Rick created *Poetry Super Highway*, an online resource and publication for poets (PoetrySuperHighway.com), *Haikuniverse*, a daily online small poem publication (Haikuniverse.com), and writes and occasionally draws the daily web comic *Cat and Banana* with Brendan Constantine (facebook.com/catandbanana). He also writes a weekly Jewish poetry column for the Los Angeles *Jewish Journal*.

Rick works as a music teacher at synagogues in Southern California and as a graphic and web designer for anyone who would like to help pay his mortgage.

Rick's Other Books and Recordings

The Low Country Shvitz
Ain't Got No Press ~ May, 2023
I Am Not Writing a Book of Poems in Hawaii
Ain't Got No Press ~ August, 2022
The Tokyo-Van Nuys Express
Ain't Got No Press ~ August, 2020
Hunka Hunka Howdee!
Ain't Got No Press ~ May, 2019

  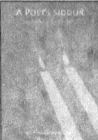 

Beautiful Mistakes
Rothco Press ~ May, 2018
17 Holy Syllables
Ain't Got No Press ~ January, 2018
A Poet's Siddur: Friday Evening (edited by)
Ain't Got No Press ~ November, 2017
God Wrestler: A Poem for Every Torah Portion
Ain't Got No Press ~ August, 2017

Donut Famine
Rothco Press ~ December, 2016
Romancing the Blarney Stone
Rothco Press ~ December, 2016
Professor Clown on Parade
Rothco Press ~ December, 2016
Rick Lupert Live and Dead (Album)
Ain't Got No Press ~ March, 2016

Making Love to the 50 Ft. Woman
Rothco Press ~ May, 2015
The Gettysburg Undress
Rothco Press ~ May, 2014
Ekphrastia Gone Wild (edited by)
Ain't Got No Press ~ July, 2013
Nothing in New England Is New
Ain't Got No Press ~ March, 2013

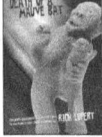   

Death of a Mauve Bat
Ain't Got No Press ~ January, 2012
The Night Goes On All Night Noir Inspired Poetry
(edited by)
Ain't Got No Press ~ November, 2011
Sinzibuckwud!
Ain't Got No Press ~ January, 2011
We Put Things in Our Mouths
Ain't Got No Press ~ January, 2010

A Poet's Haggadah (edited by)
Ain't Got No Press ~ April, 2008
A Man With No Teeth Serves Us Breakfast
Ain't Got No Press ~ May, 2007
I'd Like to Bake Your Goods
Ain't Got No Press ~ January, 2006
Stolen Mummies
Ain't Got No Press ~ February, 2003

Brendan Constantine Is My Kind of Town
Inevitable Press ~ September, 2001
Up Liberty's Skirt
Cassowary Press ~ March, 2001
Feeding Holy Cats
Cassowary Press ~ May, 2000
I'm a Jew, Are You?
Cassowary Press ~ May, 2000

Mowing Fargo
Sacred Beverage Press ~ December, 1998
Lizard King of the Laundromat
The Inevitable Press ~ February, 1998
I Am My Own Orange County
Ain't Got No Press ~ May, 1997
Paris: It's the Cheese
Ain't Got No Press ~ May, 1996

For more information:
www.PoetrySuperHighway.com

www.ingramcontent.com/pod-product-compliance
Lightning Source LLC
Chambersburg PA
CBHW052131070526
44585CB00017B/1782